PAPER GOLD
How to Hedge Against Inflation by Investing in Postage Stamps

PAPER

How to Hedge Against Inflation

KAL WAGENHEIM

by Investing in Postage Stamps

PETER H. WYDEN/Publisher/New York

Library of Congress Cataloging in Publication Data

Wagenheim, Kal.
  Paper gold.

  Includes index.
  1. Postage-stamps as an investment. I. Title.
HE6184.I5W33   332.6′722   75-32559
ISBN 0-88326-099-9

MANUFACTURED IN THE UNITED STATES OF AMERICA

Designed by Bob Antler

To my good friends
and fellow schemers and dreamers:
Gus Font,
Art Smith,
Frank Watlington,
and
Joe Guzmán.

CONTENTS

The market no longer made any sense to me.
—Gerald Supple, formerly a
$45,000-a-year Wall Street
analyst (and expert in aerospace and electronics issues),
who now runs a small bicycle
shop in Flanders, New Jersey

Phi-lat-e-ly. The collection and study of postage stamps, postmarks, and related materials; stamp collecting. From the Greek *philos* (loving) and *ateles* (tax-free), referring to the fact that postpaid letters were carried free of taxes. Literally, a *philatelist* is "a lover of tax-free things."

PAPER GOLD
How to Hedge Against Inflation by Investing in Postage Stamps

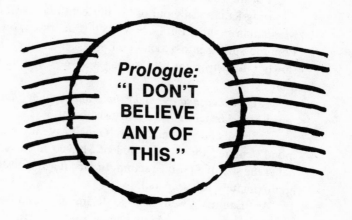

Prologue: "I DON'T BELIEVE ANY OF THIS."

"I don't believe any of this," my friend whispered, shaking his head. "I simply don't believe it."

They were bidding fast and furious at the H.R. Harmer Gallery on West Forty-Eighth Street in New York. But, looking around the room, it was hard to tell that anything was happening at all.

As Mr. Bernard Harmer conducted the bidding *("five thousand, five thousand five, six thousand...")*, the men and a few women sat quietly in their folding chairs and gazed intently at the illustrated catalogues in their laps.

Two men in the room were competing for a prized item. One smiling fellow, about forty, his eyes gleaming and his sandy hair in disarray, wore a gray and red checked jacket, green polka-dot tie and burnt-orange flare slacks. He reminded me of Gene

Wilder, the star of those mad Mel Brooks film comedies. His opponent, a few rows forward, about sixty, had a jowly pink-scrubbed face, neatly combed white hair, pearl-gray suit, and charcoal-gray tie. *He* reminded me of Edmund Wilson, the distinguished literary critic.

For the past hour, "Edmund" seemed to have been dozing or gazing lethargically out of the thirteenth-floor window at the Manhattan skyline. But now, when this item went on the block, Edmund sprang into action—well, in a genteel way, he did. He slowly raised his right fist, holding a silver-plated fountain pen aloft.

"Seven thousand . . . eight thousand . . . nine thousand," intoned Mr. Harmer in a suave British accent.

Moments later, flamboyant "Gene" gave up, and old "Edmund" entered the winning bid of $17,000 for a tiny piece of paper the size of a postage stamp. In fact, it *was* a postage stamp, approximately 106 years old.

As "Edmund" went back to dozing, my friend, who was a newcomer to stamp auctions, again said, "I refuse to believe this."

You'd better believe it. Based on its weight and value, and compared with the going rate for gold bullion, this tiny $17,000 piece of paper was worth more than $2 million per ounce.

In his youth, my friend, like myself and millions of other youngsters, had collected stamps—nickel and dime items, purchased from the weekly allowance. To many persons, collecting stamps is still "kid stuff," or a form of therapy for pensioners as they warm their bones in the Florida sunshine. But visit an auction gallery and you'll change your mind. Millions are being spent on stamps by shrewd businessmen who are intimate with the gyrations of the stock market, commodities, gold bullion and international currency exchange.

Why? Because rare stamps, over the years, have outperformed most other types of investment.

In 1975, the Ford Foundation reluctantly announced that it would have to discharge many of its employees and severely reduce its grants to scholars, because its huge investment portfolio, mainly of stocks, had shrunk in value by 45 percent. Some months before, *New York* magazine had published an entertaining piece by Dan Dorfman about "Ten Survivors of the Wall Street Crash." Gerald Supple, one of Wall Street's leading aerospace and electronic analysts, who was earning $45,000 a year, opened a small bicycle shop in New Jersey because "the market no longer made any sense to me." Pasquale Tullo, who was earning $90,000 as a specialist in new stock issues, left after fourteen years on Wall Street and opened a delicatessen in Brooklyn. Martin Ross, who had earned up to $200,000 a year as a broker and enjoyed "a model to keep my bed warm, a posh $600-a-month Manhattan pad, a Jaguar, a Mercedes, and four trips a year to Europe," was forced to get out, and opened a steak house on the upper East Side.

A doctor I know tells me, "I had $25,000 in mutual funds. I'm not an expert, but back in 1973 I had a hunch. I called my broker and said, 'Let's sell and put the money into bonds.' But he was adamant. He said that he had an even *better* mutual fund for me. Said that he was even putting his *mother's* money into it. Maybe he wanted to churn up some commissions, I don't know, but I think he was sincere. So I let him do it. My funds are worth only $9,000 today. I dropped $16,000 just like *that* [snap of fingers]. But the broker is even worse off than me. He's out of a job, and now his mother is mad at him, too."

While all of this was happening, rare-stamp values were climbing dramatically. In fact 1974, when mutual funds and stocks fell through the floor, was a banner year for the philatelic market, with some scarce items appreciating by 25 percent or more.

And if discretion appeals to you, I think it worth adding that the sale of rare stamps, unlike stocks, bonds, mutual funds, etc., can be kept quite confidential. It is also easier to store (or hide) stamps than Picassos, Tiffany lamps, coins, or even diamonds.

Stamps are not only infinitely lighter than precious metals, but they cannot be detected by electronic means. While $100,000 worth of gold weighs nearly thirty-five pounds, a similar value in rare stamps can be secreted across borders (or protected on the New York City subway) in your wallet, tucked in an envelope or, if secrecy is really your thing, taped to your leg or beneath your toupee. At home, they can be concealed behind the wall paneling of your den, between the pages of a book, behind a desk drawer, or even inside your telephone. They can be mailed across the continental United States for ten cents (a few pennies extra for registration if you wish to play it absolutely safe).

But while confidentiality can be handy, an asset is hardly "precious" (particularly in these times of inflation) unless it appreciates in value. So I think the following story will interest you.

THE UPSIDE-DOWN "JENNY"

On May 14, 1918, a man named William T. Robey waited in line at a post office in Washington, D.C. The next morning the United States was going to inaugurate airmail service between New York, Philadelphia, and Washington, using military planes to deliver the mail. The prepaid rate would be 24 cents per ounce, and the government had produced an airmail stamp in that denomination. It was an attractive red-white-blue design, which featured an engraved illustration of the then up-to-date Curtiss Jenny, a U.S. Army biplane.

When Mr. Robey's turn came, he handed $24 to the postal clerk and asked for a full sheet of 100 new stamps. Mr. Robey examined the sheet that the clerk had handed to him, and his jaw dropped. All of the Curtiss Jenny planes were flying upside-down. The lettering on the stamp was in one color, and the drawing of the plane was in another; apparently the printers had fed this sheet through the press the wrong way when they applied the second color.

There was quite a stir. A postal inspector hastened out of his office and urged Mr. Robey to surrender the odd-looking sheet of inverted stamps. But the purchaser was adamant and walked out. Briskly.

One week later, Mr. Robey sold the sheet to a Mr. Eugene Klein for $15,000—not a bad return on his original investment of $24. Actually, Mr. Klein was running a bit of a risk. At this point, he wasn't quite sure how rare the inverted Jenny might be. The government had printed 2.1 million of these 24-cent stamps, all in sheets of 100. Was this the only sheet with the plane printed upside-down? Apparently so. Much publicity was given to the $15,000 purchase, and no other specimens of the inverted Jenny ever surfaced.

Not long after that, Mr. Klein made a quick $5,000 profit, selling the precious sheet to a Col. E.H.R. Green for $20,000. Each stamp on the sheet, which had cost a mere 24 cents at the post office, was now going for $200.

Colonel Green had a flair for retailing. He divided the sheet of 100 stamps into various combinations of singles and blocks and began peddling them to wealthy collectors.

By 1925, a single stamp from the sheet was selling for about $750. In 1955, the going price was $4,000. By 1965, it was up to $12,500. And in 1974, a single copy sold at an auction in New York for $47,000. Multiply that price by the 100 stamps of the original sheet and you have the current value of Mr. Robey's original $24 investment—$4,700,000.

It's fun to think about. But such an error is so rare that one could hardly recommend waiting in line at the post office as a means of striking it rich.

However—and here's my point—even the "normal" specimen of that 24-cent stamp (issued in a quantity of 2.1 million, you'll recall) has fared beautifully as an investment. Most of them were used for postage, leaving a relatively small quantity of mint (unused) specimens for collectors. Here's how the market value of a mint specimen of the 24-cent Curtiss Jenny stamp of 1918 has climbed over the years:

1925 .... $ .35		1955 .... $ 3.95	
1935 .... .95		1965 .... 7.25	
1945 .... 2.00		1975 .... 38.50	

As you can see, had you purchased one (or several) of these in 1965, the value of your investment would have quintupled in the past decade. While this stamp appreciated by over 500 percent over the past ten years, the average stock or mutual fund grew by only 35 percent.

At this point, if you're unfamiliar with the world of philately, you may have a few questions. Three may come to mind immediately:

Q. *Do all stamps behave in this manner?*

A. Emphatically not.

Q. *But have a number of stamps appreciated in value over the years at a rate superior to bank savings, stocks and mutual funds?*

A. Emphatically yes.

Q. *Is there a way to determine which go up and which don't?*

A. There is a simple method of charting the past performance of stamps, enabling you to discard the majority of stamps that either stand still or appreciate in value too slowly to attract the investor. Unlike stocks and mutual funds, the overwhelming majority of truly scarce stamps (and I'll define this later) tend to behave as they have in the past. So the answer is a qualified, but emphatic, yes.

WHAT THIS BOOK CAN DO FOR YOU

This book will demonstrate that stamp investment is an attractive alternative (or supplement) to more conventional forms of investment (stocks, bonds, funds, gold bullion, etc.), most of which involve greater risk and have yielded less generous profits.

Many thousands of persons all over the world invest in stamps. If you have never done so, this book will show you how to identify a stamp with investment potential, how to acquire it at a sensible price, and how to sell it for maximum gain. If you already invest in stamps, you may find that the information contained in this book strongly challenges the rationale of your "game plan"; you may want to question whether or not your investments are based on sound principles; or, even if they are, whether you could be doing even better.

Certain rare stamps have been appreciating in value by 15 percent per year, no matter whether Wall Street is in a bullish or bearish mood. Have you identified the right ones? Are you paying a proper price for them?

This book will help you to answer these and other basic questions.

SETTING THE RECORD STRAIGHT

Before proceeding further, I'd like to set the record straight on a matter of principle. Perhaps you have read (or heard of) recent best-selling books by Harry Browne: *How to Profit from the Coming Devaluation,* and *You Can Profit from a Monetary Crisis.*

In these books, Mr. Browne recommends that the reader protect himself against "America's worst Depression" by purchasing gold and silver coins, and other precious metals. He also recommends setting up a remote hideaway, and stocking it with food, in order to isolate one's self from urban riots when the economy plunges through the floor. I am much less pessimistic than Mr. Browne. I think that our economy is resilient enough to avoid such extreme crises. I do believe that certain rare collectibles such as coins and stamps (the right ones, at the right price) make sense as a hedge against inflation and a means of building your equity over the long term.

Mr. Browne, in his books, frequently recommends one coin supplier, The Pacific Coast Coin Exchange, as a source of investment material.

In December 1974, the Securities and Exchange Commission filed a complaint against Pacific Coast Coin Exchange, charging it with fraud. According to *The New York Times* (March 29, 1975, page 30):

> The S.E.C. complaint said that the supplier used hard-sell, fraudulent methods, charged "exorbitant" fees for services it never performed and fixed silver prices arbitrarily to the customers' detriment.
>
> Scare tactics and doom-and-gloom forecasts were used, the S.E.C. charged, to attract customers who were then sold more contracts than they could afford. . . . The supplier neither admitted nor denied the charges but consented to a restraining order prohibiting fraudulent and deceptive acts and the future sale of coins on margin . . .

While Mr. Browne himself was not charged with any violation of the securities law, the S.E.C. did report that he was once the marketing director of the Pacific Coast Coin Exchange, and that he received a commission for every customer he brought in to the Pacific Coast Coin Exchange. As a result, says the *Times,* "Mr. Browne collected more than $100,000." The article adds:

> Mr. Browne is not the first individual to write a book or recommend a supplier or brokerage house without disclosing an association. But to some, Mr. Browne's ties with the coin supplier were more questionable than in many such cases.

To set the record straight, I would like to state that in this book, while I mention the names of numerous sources of rare stamps, I do so merely as a point of information to the reader. I have dealt with many of them, and found their services to be quite satisfactory, but I am in no position to recommend them. Furthermore, I am in no way affiliated with any of them, and will derive no gain from transactions involving them and readers of this book.

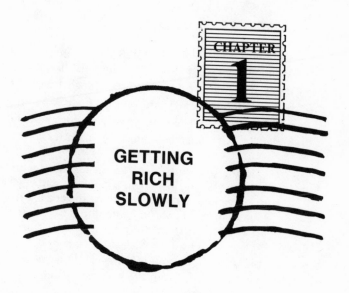

**GETTING
RICH
SLOWLY**

If you are seeking a simplistic get-rich-quick formula in these pages, I suggest that you stop reading this minute. Such schemes don't exist in any field of investment, and only poor, gullible souls believe that they do. John Train, a professional manager of investments for the wealthy, says in his recent book, *Dance of the Money Bees:*

> The alpha and omega of investment is preservation of capital in real terms. It is a very respectable objective, rarely attained. Let the reader approach portfolio investment in that spirit, and perhaps he will do much better. If he tries for miracles, he will probably do worse.

The preservation of capital in real terms: what, exactly, does that mean?

Since 1940, the purchasing power of the U.S. dollar has dwindled by nearly two-thirds. Since 1960, the Consumer Price Index has gone up by 62 percent. Such basic items as bread, bacon, gasoline, dental care, and the price of a movie ticket—as I probably need not remind you—have gone up even higher. In mid-1974, syndicated columnist Sylvia Porter lamented:

> Right now, with the cost of living rising at an utterly intolerable rate, just about any investment gives you a negative rate of return—meaning the erosion from today's inflation, plus the bite from taxes more than eat up what you earn in interest.

And *U.S. News & World Report,* in a study of investment alternatives, asked aloud: "Where can a family put its savings with some hope of protecting them against a steady decline in the dollar?" In effect, the magazine threw in the towel, concluding that the best a family can do is hold its losses to a minimum by judicious investing.

This is not just a local phenomenon. In 1974, while U.S. inflation was moving ahead so that the purchasing power of the dollar was being cut by 11 percent per year (compared with 2.5 percent in 1972), inflation was roaring along at 25 percent in Japan, 18 percent in Italy and 14.5 percent in Great Britain.

As for the future, the *Kiplinger Washington Letter* sees "boom and inflation ahead," with inflation likely to "gallop along at nearly twice the rate of the 1960s . . . despite all efforts to roll it back."

"Whether you look at it for the short run or the long run," says James J. O'Leary, vice chairman of the United States Trust Company of New York, "we've got a chronic problem with inflation."

HOW COLLECTIBLES BEAT INFLATION

Let us suppose, then, that inflation stabilizes at about 10 percent yearly. This means that just to break even in buying power, you must earn 15 percent a year on your investments, if you are in the 33 percent tax bracket. And if you are in the 50 percent tax bracket, you must earn 20 percent per year just to preserve capital "in real terms."

No bank can offer such a yield. And the types of stocks and funds that offer potential for such vigorous appreciation are loaded with risk. That is why astute individuals in the upper-income brackets include in their investment portfolios a heavy component of collectibles (fine art, antiques, rare coins, and stamps), many of which have managed to stay a few steps ahead of inflation.

Let's take a specific example. In 1902, a set of sixteen U.S. stamps known as the Columbian Issue of 1893 was valued at $19.50 in mint condition. By 1970, due to inflation, one needed $120 to have purchasing power equivalent to the $19.50 of 1902. However, by 1970, the same set of Columbian stamps was worth about $1,800. In other words, these rare stamps had far, far more than just kept pace with inflation over a period of seven decades.

While their cumulative growth has been spectacular, these Columbian stamps did not grow by sensational overnight leaps. They appreciated steadily, from year to year, building and compounding, usually at better than 10 percent yearly—between 1974 and 1975, they grew in value by 19 percent.

That is why I concur with the philosophy of stamp investment broker Jeffrey L. Needleman of Brooklyn, who says:

> The chances of getting rich at all are slim. And the chances of getting rich quickly are minuscule. . . . Those who got rich on their own made money slowly,

deliberately and consistently over a period of years. . . .
Luckily, you don't have to get rich quickly to get
rich . . .

WHAT THE EXPERTS SAY

Norman S. Hubbard, a professor of economics at Brooklyn
College, regards rare stamps in top condition as "blue chip investments," and estimates that "an average annual rate of return
of eight to ten percent is attainable." On the basis of 10 percent
gain, an investment of $10,000 today would be worth $25,000 in a
decade, and about $63,000 in two decades.

Lately, the return has been even better. During the "bullish"
period of the stock market, the kind we saw during the economic
boom of the middle and late 1960s, rare stamps were appreciating at the rate of 15 percent yearly, meaning that $10,000 in-
vested would be worth $30,000 in a decade, and about $90,000 in
two.

In 1970, commenting on the boom period, *Forbes* magazine said: "If you think the stock market was running wild with
speculation in 1968 and 1969, take a look at what's going on in
postage-stamp collecting." The prices for rare stamps, *Forbes*
continued,

> have been rising year to year, without pause, at an
> annual rate of between 10 percent and 25 percent.
> What these figures mean is that prices have been going
> up somewhere between 150 percent and 800 percent
> every decade. Thus, a $10,000 stamp today could be
> expected to be worth somewhere between $25,000 and
> $90,000 by 1980. . . . In 1960, it might well have been
> selling for somewhere between $100 and $400.

Keep these figures in mind when you contemplate strategies
to finance your children's college education, or your own
retirement.

Business Week in 1971 touched upon another aspect worth noting:

> In these days of floating currencies, there's an added lure for the stamp collector–investor. The value of a collection of foreign stamps fluctuates in the same way as the value of foreign currency. So, for example, a classic collection of German stamps would now fetch 10 percent more dollars than it would have early this year.

COMPARING STAMPS WITH OTHER INVESTMENTS

Let's take a ten-year perspective. Suppose that in 1963 you had divided $4,000 into equal shares and invested it in a variety of ways. Here's how each $1,000 would have performed by 1973, a decade later:

Savings accounts, at 5 percent interest	$1,630
Mutual funds (a representative sampling)	1,683
Dow Jones Industrial stocks	1,283
Rare (pre-1920) U.S. postage stamps	4,250

During that ten-year period, while the cost of living rose 44 percent, rare stamps grew in value by more than 300 percent. Bank savings and mutual funds grew by slightly more than 60 percent, and common stocks rose by 28 percent, not even keeping pace with the rate of inflation.

There were given moments during the decade when stocks and funds performed brilliantly, but their values were crippled by downturns in the economy. During the eighteen-month recession in 1969-70, the consumer price index rose 9 percent and Dow Jones Industrial stocks dropped by 36 percent. In that same period, rare stamps registered a 33 percent gain.

This brings us to another fascinating point. When the market turned decidedly bearish in the 1970s, stock values fell, prices soared, and massive job layoffs signalled that we were in the midst of a serious recession—but rare stamp values really took off.

During 1974, the value of stocks and mutual funds dropped by about 6 percent, and even the sale of fine art was slumping. That was the best year in the entire history of the Harmer organization, which sold $6.75 million worth of rare stamps at its auction galleries in London, New York, and Sydney, an increase of $1.2 million over the previous year. A California firm that has made a computerized study of stamp auction prices across the country for the past dozen years reported that increases in value during 1974 were "on the average more than twice as great as those reported in any previous year."

In summary, stamps performed well in the boom years of the 1960s, and even better in the bust period of the 1970s.

HOW STAMPS BEAT RECESSIONS

Why? Are stamps "recession-proof"? No one can foretell future events, but the past provides some clues.

During the Great Depression of the 1930s, stamps retained their value quite tenaciously. One major stamp dealer, discussing the motivations of some of his clients, says:

> Many of them tell me their fathers or uncles had stamps to sell during the 1930s. They all remember they were able to sell their stamps for cash, along with grandma's diamond ring, while few other assets were convertible into money. It's a funny thing; this has an effect on people years later.

Persons familiar with philately also recall the time in 1930, when the estate of Arthur Hind, a very wealthy man, was liquidated. His stocks and bonds returned only a fraction of their original cost, but his stamp collection sold for hundreds of thousands of dollars more than his original outlay.

Jacques Minkus, one of the big names in the stamp world (he is the publisher of the Minkus catalogues and albums), got his *start* right in the midst of the Great Depression—in 1931, when other businesses were folding. He went to Gimbels Department Store in Manhattan and started with six feet of counter space. His friends thought he was crazy. After forty-three years, the stamp department now dominates a good part of Gimbels' first floor, its yearly gross is in seven figures, and Minkus has spread out to dozens of locations across the country.

Recalling his early years, Mr. Minkus says: "Stockbrokers on their way home via the Penn Station would stop in and ask me for something to take their minds off the happenings of the time. I would start them on the joy of collecting."

It wasn't only joy that lured some of those stockbrokers into his stamp store. Stamps (and other precious collectibles) represent an entirely different phenomenon from stocks, which are tied to the state of the economy. Even in good times, a number of stocks plummet in value because of corporate mismanagement or changing technology that makes one company's product more competitive than another's. But the quantity of a rare stamp never increases. It is finite. Meanwhile, the legion of collectors continues to grow, thus creating a constantly strong demand. And when Wall Street turns bearish, a lot of non-philatelic money abandons the stock market and seeks a safe haven in collectibles, thus driving the price of stamps even higher.

AN EXAMPLE: THE $5 COLUMBIAN

Let's take the example of an item well known to collectors of U.S. stamps, the $5 black Columbian of 1893. This stamp was issued by the post office more than eighty years ago, in a total quantity of 27,350. Many were used for postage and later discarded. Let us make a generous estimate and suppose that about 7,000 exist in mint condition. Match that 7,000 against several million collectors—all of whom own albums that contain an illustrated space to be filled by this $5 stamp—and you will see why it has risen in value at such a dramatic pace.

In 1965 the value of the $5 Columbian (in fine, unused condition) was $170. By 1970 it was worth $450. Four years later it was up to $775. Now it is valued at $900. In other words, that stamp went up in value by 16 percent in a year, 100 percent in five years, and 429 percent in ten years. This is not an isolated case. I will cite many others in future chapters.

HOW I BECAME A STAMP INVESTOR

If this is your first exposure to the possibilities of stamp investment, perhaps you'd be interested in how I first became aware of their potential.

In the mid-1960s, I was living in San Juan, Puerto Rico, where I worked as political correspondent for *The New York Times* and edited a local magazine. I had also just completed the manuscript of a history book about Puerto Rico, after several months of hard labor on evenings and weekends.

Late one morning, after mailing the manuscript to my publisher in New York, I drove around town, planning to kill a bit of time before meeting a friend for lunch. I felt elated, keyed up, and—oddly—a bit empty. Although the book was done, my mind still raced ahead, spurred on by the momentum of my hard work of the past few months.

At times like those, after finishing an arduous project, I find that "busy work," occupying myself, without taxing my mind too heavily, is a nice antidote. I suspect that a number of lovely flower gardens have been planted and nurtured for the same reason.

As I drove around San Juan, I spotted a sign saying *Sellos Para Coleccionistas* ("Stamps for Collectors").

I still can't say what made me park the car and go in. The last time I had looked at a postage stamp album was during my grammar school days. That was still in the era of radio, and on winter evenings I enjoyed listening to Eddie Cantor, Jack Benny, *The Shadow,* and all those marvelous old shows, at the same time toying around with an inexpensive beginner's album, pasting in colorful stamps from such exotic places as Tannu-Tuva, Bechuanaland, and Sierra Leone. It was fun, and I learned a great deal of geography. I've since learned more: The price markup on those stamps was enormous, and my collection, which consisted primarily of cancelled stamps that were available in huge quantities, was virtually worthless for resale.

But who, after all, can put a price on pleasure?

Don Carlos, the proprietor of the stamp store in San Juan, was a Spaniard in his early sixties. White-haired, stocky, stern-looking, he had lived in Havana until the Castro Revolution, and then moved to Puerto Rico.* His store measured about twelve by twelve feet, with a small glass counter, and wall shelves from floor to ceiling, crammed with albums, stock books, and cardboard boxes. I was the only customer.

I speak Spanish and, after glancing around the shop for a moment, told Don Carlos that I was "looking for an album, and perhaps a beginner's packet of stamps, for my son." I was still too embarrassed to admit that *I* had an interest in them myself! After a few minutes' discussion, I decided to buy a quality "specialized" album of the Latin West Indies, which included the stamps of Cuba, Dominican Republic, Haiti, and Puerto Rico. I also bought a few dollars' worth of stamps.

That night, at home, I enjoyed a few hours of sorting the stamps and hinging them into the album, as my wife and a writer friend who dropped by wondered aloud if I had slipped into a "second childhood" that is usually associated with senility. The stamps were lovely multicolored engravings, most of them from the nineteenth century, and I went back for more a few days later. Within a few weeks, Don Carlos and I were friends. Since

---

* Stamp collecting, by the way, is not strictly a "capitalist hobby." There are many philatelists in Cuba. And I am told that the Soviet Union has more stamp clubs per capita than the United States.

his English was rather limited, and he occasionally got requests in the mail from collectors in the United States, I helped him translate the letters and draft his replies.

As the weeks slipped by, certain doubts began to develop. During the many hours that I spent in Don Carlos' shop, only a handful of customers came by, some of them school children who spent only a dollar or two. My own purchases were quite modest, five or ten dollars at a time. What in hell, I asked myself, was Don Carlos doing for a living?

THE SECRET OF DON CARLOS

I finally gathered enough confidence to broach this matter delicately with him. I took a circuitous route, first complaining about the high cost of living. I brought up the question of rent, light bills, air conditioning. Did he run his business at a loss?

He smiled, then pointed to the boxes and albums crammed onto the shelves, and at the large safe in the back room.

"Young man," he said, "I began collecting some forty years ago. Many of these stamps were picked up for next to nothing. They are worth a fortune today!

"I do a large mail-order business and gradually sell off my stock. Even by offering a big discount I clear a good profit.

"In about five years, I'll retire, close this shop, and continue my business at home. Whenever I need a little cash, all I have to do is place an ad in the paper, or consign some of my stamps to auctions. It's just like clipping stock coupons.

"I also do a lot of business you don't see. There are several professional men—doctors, lawyers, dentists—who invest in stamps through me. They buy whole sheets of sets of rare stamps, a few hundred dollars at a time, and put them away in the bank for safe keeping. Every so often they call me, place an order, and come by my home in the evening to pick up the stamps. I make a nice profit, and they now have a good investment, which keeps growing year by year."

Every stamp collector, even a young child, has in the back of his mind that stamps are worth "something," and could over the years be worth even more. That is part of the magic of collecting. But this was the first time, at the ripe age of thirty, that the investment potential of stamps really hit home. Until then, stamps were for mounting in albums. But some men were storing them in the bank! I immediately besieged Don Carlos with questions. *Which* stamps were good investments?

Chuckling, he said, "You have to know what you're doing."

Could he mention just a *few* good stamps for investment? (Only now, in retrospect, do I realize how silly I must have looked and sounded.)

"Israel," he whispered conspiratorially. "Some of their earlier ones, in full sheets." He mentioned a few others. Looking back from the perspective of more than a decade, I can see how right he was.

It was then that I began to collect in earnest. And to regard stamps as something more than attractive snips of paper.

A few years later, I moved from Puerto Rico back to the mainland United States. I have continued to study the stamp market, and to invest. As a writer, my income has been somewhat uncertain. But I have purchased stamps regularly. Many of them, acquired a few years ago, are far more valuable today. I have already sold a few for good profit. But my primary goal is to accumulate more, and allow them to appreciate over the long haul.

HOW STAMPS DIFFER FROM OTHER INVESTMENTS

Stamps are so different from more conventional types of investment that you may not be temperamentally suited to make the change to philately. Let's explore some of these differences so you can assess for yourself just how you feel about them.

First of all, consider the very nature of stamp investment and contrast it with other options. When you purchase a common stock, you receive a certificate or a receipt which, in itself, has no value. It symbolizes a share in the future activities of a corporation. Your fortunes will rise and fall in accord with the success of a company that makes business machines, pencils, missiles, diapers, or hamburgers. I don't mean to be critical. I merely wish to point out that when you buy stocks you are primarily concerned with the value of your shares and need not "relate" to the nature of the corporations that you partly own. It is strictly a financial transaction.

When you buy a painting by Picasso or an exquisite Tiffany lamp or a rare postage stamp, you possess it totally. You do not have a receipt that represents partial ownership in some vast, anonymous enterprise. Speaking personally, and rather subjectively, I happen to prefer total possession of my investment assets, and I enjoy the fact that, in addition to their monetary value, they are esthetically pleasing. Whether or not this makes any difference to *you* is something that only you can answer.

Then there is the question of fluctuation of values, the matter of pace. Stocks and mutual funds can rise and fall in a matter of minutes; the price movement of stamps is glacial by comparison. If you are the type of person who must be constantly so involved that you cannot resist calling your broker every day or two, you had best stay away from stamps. (There is plenty of excitement to be had in philately, however, particularly at auctions, which I'll discuss later.)

The price markup on stamps is relatively high, although if you make a major purchase you might keep it down to the equivalent of what you'd pay in mutual fund commissions. It takes time for stamps to appreciate above the markup. If you are an obsessively "action-oriented" person who thrives on constant turnover of your investment portfolio, you are unsuited for stamps, because you will constantly be inflicting losses upon yourself. In fact, you are probably unsuited for any type of investment if you let your passions interfere with sound business sense.

"Don't look for short-term gain," says Greg Manning, the head of a large stamp company in South Orange, New Jersey. "I usually tell people not to worry about values for five years at least."

The difference in scale between the stock and stamp markets is also worth noting. The major stock exchanges in the United States handle several billion dollars a day in transactions. The American stamp market is minuscule by comparison, handling perhaps a couple of billion dollars per year.

On March 25, 1975, a New York stamp auction gallery—Robert A. Siegel—sold a million dollars' worth of stamps in a single day; it was the first time this has happened in U.S. history. Which helps explain why stamp values soared when some non-philatelic money flowed out of Wall Street and into stamps.

HOW STAMP PRICES ARE SET

The price structure of the market must also be taken into consideration. While you can pick up the phone and call a brokerage house to inquire about the price of any stock, certain collectibles, such as fine art or antiques, some of which are unique, may be traded only once every few years. Due to this infrequency, the market price at a given time depends largely upon intuition and insider's knowledge of the market.

Stamps are somewhere in the middle between these two extremes. They are traded frequently, every day in fact; reports on prices are not as immediately available as stocks, but by merely perusing advertisements in the stamp weeklies, you can arrive at a ballpark figure for a particular property.

Another factor influencing your choice of any investment is liquidity. Hard cash is, of course, the most liquid of assets. Perhaps the least liquid is real estate, which can take years to be converted into a satisfying amount of cash. Gold bullion, stocks, and bonds are nearly as liquid as cash, because they can be converted in a day or two. Russell S. Bell, a California stamp dealer, calls stamps "semi-liquid," a term that I like. As he says, "You *can* sell in a day or two ... but you may get but a small fraction of what you could realize if you had a few weeks or months to explore the marketplace."

I will explain later how to get quick cash for your stamps, without being fleeced.

HOW TO WEIGH INVESTMENT RISKS

Risk is another factor. While no one can be absolutely sure of the future, certain investments are—by their very nature—more vulnerable to risk than others. I believe, for example, that gold and silver bullion are overrated. Their price is based on current and anticipated world supplies. But *their supply is not finite.* More gold and silver can be mined, or vast existing amounts that are hoarded can be suddenly dumped on the market, which would depress the value of your holdings. And remember: This is entirely beyond your control.

Stocks, too, are beyond your control. When you invest in stocks, you are, in effect, giving a vote of confidence to the talent and character of corporate executives whom you don't know. You are also "betting" that the products or services they market will remain competitive. We've already seen how stocks and mutual funds "crashed" in 1974. If a company fails, your entire investment can vanish. Furthermore, major blocks of shares are controlled by a few large institutional investors. Their buy and sell decisions have a tremendous impact upon stock prices. The small investor has no control over these phenomena, and must remain constantly alert for sudden dips and leaps in the market.

Stamps (and other rare collectibles) are not subject to sudden impact. The vast majority are dispersed among many individual collectors. No single dealer—not even a handful of major dealers—can corner the market on a rare stamp. In fact, dealers are constantly and eagerly advertising to *buy* stamps, so that they can resell them at a profit to their collector clientele. Because the stamp market is so unorganized in comparison with stocks, it is just about impossible to tinker with the price structure. So the small investor is infinitely better protected. Supply and demand, not corporate incompetence or tricky maneuvering by insiders, govern the value of stamps.

TAX ADVANTAGES

When the time comes to sell, you must also consider the impact of taxes. Dividends and interest from stocks and bank savings are subject to ordinary income tax each year. Providing you hold on to your stamps for at least six months, any profits you derive from their resale are treated under the more favorable capital gains tax. As you know, the factor of "after-tax" gain can be immensely important if you are in the upper-middle or upper tax bracket.

Another factor—less tangible, I admit—that appeals to me is the diffidence of stamp dealers. Rarely, in conversation or in printed advertisements, will they allude to the investment value of their products.

Earl Apfelbaum, a well-known dealer in Philadelphia, urges collectors to acquire stamps for pleasure, and only admits with a bit of prodding that "better grade stamps can be financially rewarding."

Not long ago, I sent an inquiry to Raymond H. Weill, who heads a prestigious rare stamp firm in New Orleans. He replied:

"We have always hesitated to give opinions about the advisability of investing in rare stamps. We could easily be accused of favoring, because we are involved, and naturally we would hardly take an opposite view, since we ourselves invest heavily."

But, as Don Carlos warned, "You have to know what you're doing."

That's the subject of the next chapter.

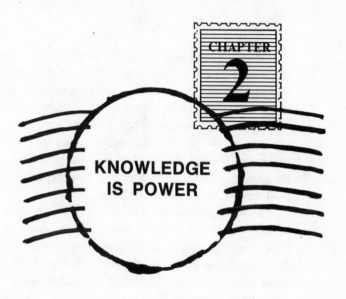

KNOWLEDGE
IS POWER

In any field of investment, knowledge is power. Many people, operating on the basis of blind faith in some "market messiah," have tossed away fortunes on wild schemes. With rare exceptions, profits are the result of prudent choice that limits risk to a minimum.

There is a wealth of source material on philately to help you acquire the knowledge that is essential to wise investment. You will find these data in books, magazines, newspapers, catalogues, and price lists. One needn't be an "insider"; it is all there, available to anyone who has the patience to do a bit of studying.

In fact, there is so much information available that it can drive you dizzy. With time, however, your interests will narrow to some specialty, and you will need fewer sources (and fewer hours) to stay abreast of new developments.

Keeping informed needn't be an all-consuming task. As I've mentioned before, stamp values change at a leisurely pace, and you needn't pay feverish attention to market fluctuations, provided that you've chosen a wise investment policy from the start.

Much depends, too, upon what type of collector/investor you wish to be. In the stock market, some investors allow their brokers to handle everything, while others are avid students of the game, and constantly pore over newspapers, magazines, annual reports, and market tip sheets.

Stamps offer the same flexibility. You can allow a dealer or broker to make all of the decisions, or you can buy and sell on your own. It depends upon your own personality, and how much time you have available. As we have repeatedly seen in the stock market, it can be perilous to trust brokers 100 percent. Their loyalty to you is compromised by their natural desire to buy and sell and achieve turnover to earn commissions and more commissions. Also, no matter how honest they may be, they can be dead wrong. Even if you do allow someone else to handle your stamp investment portfolio, it would be reckless not to become familiar with the world of philately.

A USEFUL NOTE FROM HISTORY

How did it all begin?

In 1837, Sir Rowland Hill of England proposed a new idea to reform the country's postal service. Until then, fees for delivering letters were usually paid by the recipient. Postal rates were high, and varied widely from place to place. Payment was noted by rubber stamp or handwritten markings.

Sir Rowland suggested a uniform prepaid rate of one penny for all inland letters, no matter the distance involved. He suggested that postage prepayment be made "by using a bit of paper just large enough to bear the stamp (design) and covered at the back with a glutinous wash."

Three years later, England adopted his idea and instituted the world's first postage stamp, now popularly known as The Penny Black of 1840. This simply designed stamp featured an engraved portrait of Queen Victoria. Since pre-Roman times coins had always shown the head of an empire's reigning monarch, and the stamp, in a sense, was regarded as a type of paper coin.

Within a few years, nations all over the world adopted the idea of prepaid postage and stamps with "a glutinous wash" on the back so that they could easily be affixed to the envelope. By the late 1840s, the United States also adopted the practice, but —since it was not a monarchy—portraits of such leaders as Benjamin Franklin, George Washington and Thomas Jefferson adorned this nation's earliest stamps.

The idea of collecting stamps got started and caught on very quickly. There was something exotic, particularly in the nineteenth century, about a tiny engraving that had traveled across the country, or halfway around the globe, and whose postmarks hinted at the romance of faraway places.

In 1869, the United States modified the tradition of portraying only national leaders on its stamps and issued its first Pictorial Series. The series included portraits of Washington, Franklin and Lincoln, but there were also illustrations of a post horse and rider, a locomotive, a ship, an eagle perched on the national shield, and scenes that depicted the landing of Columbus and the signing of the Declaration of Independence.

Obviously, stamps were becoming miniature posters that reflected a nation's history and ideals. At about that time, a thoughtful assistant postmaster general in Washington wrote a letter to his printers, complaining about the drab colors of a newly produced stamp:

> As this stamp is to be sent abroad, it should be at least equal in brilliancy to any of the others now in use. It may not have occurred to you, but it is nevertheless

true that by many persons of education and taste the good fame of great nations, as relates to the arts, rests upon such small things as postage stamps.

Soon, as stamp collecting burgeoned into a hobby of international scope, there arose a need to codify the rapidly increasing number of stamps, and to establish widely acceptable values for them. Two of the pioneers in these efforts were Edward Stanley Gibbons of England, and John Walter Scott, who is considered to be "the father of American philately."

Gibbons was born in 1840—the same year the Penny Black was first issued—in a flat above his father's pharmacy on Treville Street in Plymouth, England. By 1854, when both philately and Gibbons were young, he had already accumulated a tiny collection of stamps. When his brother William died the next year, Edward took his place as an "apprentice in pills and powders." Between prescriptions, he also bought and sold stamps from a desk in the corner of the shop. Soon, the stamp firm of E. Stanley Gibbons was taking in more money than the pharmacy. By 1865, he was publishing a monthly price list.

Two years later, on the other side of the Atlantic, John Walter Scott also began to issue monthly price lists for his growing stamp business. In September of 1868, Scott printed his first "descriptive catalogue of American and foreign postage stamps," which included items issued "from 1840 to date."

This twenty-one-page catalogue, which sold for 15 cents, is now a collector's item. Among its many offerings was the 5-cent brown U.S. stamp of 1847, at 5 cents for a used specimen—the present value is $135. In 1870, Scott is said to have conducted the first stamp auction in the United States, and two years later held the first in England, at Sotheby's.

By 1887, he devised a system of identifying stamps that is known today as "Scott numbering." Anywhere in the United States, and in most parts of the world, a stamp is readily identified by its *Scott Catalogue* number. For example, in referring to the first stamp issued by the United States, in 1847, a 5-cent red-brown portrait of Benjamin Franklin, you need merely say, "U.S. number one."

By then, Gibbons had long moved his flourishing stamp business to London. He, too, had devised a catalogue numbering system, which is widely used, particularly in Europe and in British Commonwealth nations, and referred to as "Gibbons numbering."

The Scott and the Gibbons firms have since blossomed into huge corporations. They not only issue price catalogues but also manufacture albums, magazines and other philatelic accessories. Although Scott and Gibbons stand out as the twin giants of this global hobby, many others have played important roles in its development. Some families have been involved for generations in the management of prestigious auction galleries or stamp firms. Brilliant artists and engravers have contributed their talents to the design of stamps. Monarchs, presidents and other major personalities on the world scene formed splendid collections that now reside in museums. Scholars have made specialized studies of postal history, of the changes in printing technology used to issue stamps, and other aspects of philately.

HOW TO SPEAK STAMP LANGUAGE

People in all walks of life—astronauts, stockbrokers, sociologists, bookies—have their own special language. So do stamp people.

Basic stamp language is fairly simple, and it is *essential* to learn it if you contemplate becoming a collector/investor.* Here

---

* I use the term "collector/investor" because I regard the two words as inseparable. In order to make sensible stamp investments, your knowledge should at least be equivalent to that of the average collector, and preferably it should be superior. Not only will this pay off monetarily, but it will enable you to enjoy the search for, and acquisition of, your investment properties.

is a brief glossary—a quickie Berlitz course. As you become familiar with the various stamp publications, your vocabulary will grow further.

A *stamp* is a small piece of paper with a design printed on the front and, in most cases, adhesive gum applied on the back. Stamps are usually printed in a *sheet* of a few hundred from a *plate*. Many recent U.S. stamps, for example, are printed in sheets of 200 identical subjects. Before delivery to post offices, the sheet is divided into *panes*. A sheet of 200 stamps is commonly divided into four panes of 50 stamps apiece. When you ask your postal clerk for a "sheet" of stamps, he will actually be giving you a "pane" (no pun intended). You should be aware of the difference. Most ads that offer to buy or sell stamps by the "sheet" are actually referring to a "pane."

In most cases, the *design* of a stamp is framed by a white border, or *margin*. The word "margin" can also refer to the border around a pane or sheet of stamps.

Many years ago, stamps were printed on sheets and then rather crudely cut apart by scissors. Methods were then devised to separate them easily. One method was known as *rouletting*. This entailed cutting short incisions into the paper, at intervals, between the rows of stamps. Someone else devised a method of *perforation:* Tiny holes, spaced close together, were punched between the rows of stamps. The remaining bits of paper that link perforated stamps to each other are known as *perforation teeth*.

Some stamps appear identical, but have what is called a different *perforation gauge*. If, for example, a stamp is said to be "Perf 12," this means that twelve perforations can be counted in a two-centimeter length along the top edge of the stamp. Don't worry, you won't have to count them; perforation gauge measures are available for a few pennies. A stamp described as "Perf 13½" has that many perforations in the same two-centimeter stretch. This factor is unimportant in the case of the many stamps that are produced with identical perforation measures. But in some cases stamps of similar design and color have different measures and vary in scarcity, which affects their market value.

A stamp not separated by perforations, either by design or due to error, is said to be *imperforate*. A *straight edge,* often denoted as "SE" in auction catalogues, refers to a stamp that has three perforated sides and one side that is imperforate. This occurs when the outer edge of a sheet of stamps is not perforated; copies on the margin will have at least one straight edge, and those in the corners will have two straight edges. Many of the early stamps of the United States and Canada were printed in this fashion.

Four or more joined stamps, at least two high and two wide, are known as a *block*. Rarer, and more expensive than the common block, is the *margin block* bearing a plate number; this is usually referred to as a *plate block*. A common block can be formed from any part of a sheet of stamps. A plate block comes from the corner of the pane, and includes the printed number of the sheet in the adjoining margin. Most plate blocks consist of four stamps, but others are commonly collected in blocks of six, or blocks of ten (your Scott catalogue will tell you which ones).

A *single* is, of course, one stamp. A *plate number single* is one stamp, attached to a margin that shows the plate number of the sheet. A *pair* refers to two unsevered stamps. A *strip* means three or more stamps, joined together either horizontally or vertically. When stamps that vary in design or value are printed on the same sheet, a pair of these different items joined together is called *se-tenant*.

Stamps printed in long continuous strips and sold in roll form are called *coils.* If these stamps are joined together at the sides, they will be imperforate at top and bottom; if they are linked at top and bottom, they are imperforate on both sides. A *coil pair* means, simply, two joined coil stamps. A *line pair* occurs in the rotary printing process, when the curved rotary plates meet or join on the press, creating a line of color between some stamps on the coil. These are much rarer than run-of-the-mill line pairs and command higher prices. A *booklet pane* is a miniature sheet of stamps, printed in this format for sale in booklets. The outer edges of the stamps on the perimeter of the pane are imperforate.

A *cover* refers to the envelope, or wrapper, used to mail a letter. A *stampless cover* is just that, and usually dates back to the era before stamps were used, when postal clerks cancelled the envelope with a handwritten notation or manually applied rubber stamp. Envelopes, postcards, and other items that have stamps printed or embossed on them are known as *postal stationery*. A stamp is *tied on* to its cover when the cancellation mark appears partly on the stamp and partly on the envelope.

A *first day cover,* usually called an FDC, is an envelope that bears a stamp cancelled on the same day the stamp was issued, often at the city designated as the site of issue. A *cachet* is a specially printed envelope, used to "dress up" the first day issue with a design and text that tells the story behind the stamp's design, or explains the event that the stamp is commemorating.

A *commemorative* is a stamp issued for a limited time, to honor some person, theme or event. A *definitive* is a stamp issued for regular postal use, and is usually smaller and more simply designed; it frequently has a "life" of several years, until postal rates go up, thus requiring definitive stamps with higher values.

An *essay* is the artist's original design for a stamp, which was submitted for the approval of the postal authorities and not accepted. A *proof* is a trial printing of a stamp, to check color, design, the quality of the plate, etc. A *die proof* is a proof taken from the original die upon which the stamp design was engraved.

A STAMP'S CONDITION IS CRUCIAL

The condition of a stamp depends upon several factors. First of all, a *used* stamp is one which has passed through the mails and, in most cases, shows a cancellation mark. An *unused* stamp has not been employed for postage. Beware of the difference between *unused* and *mint*. A mint stamp is an unused stamp that is in pristine post office condition. For example, if a mint stamp is mounted in an album with a paper hinge, it is no longer mint. When you remove the hinge, you also pull off some of the original gum (og) from the back of the stamp, and leave a *hinge mark*. A truly mint stamp is one that is *never-hinged* (NH). An unused stamp may be *lightly hinged* (LH), *very lightly hinged* (VLH) or *heavily hinged* (HH). It may be so heavily hinged that there are *hinge remnants* (HR) encrusted on the back of the stamp. Many ads offer mint stamps but, in reality, deliver unused stamps. Read their offers carefully. This is important, because a large premium is often paid for early stamps that are NH.

A stamp's condition is probably the single most important factor in its market value. Condition is judged on the basis of a stamp's *centering* (the even width of the margins around the design), its freshness of color, its crisp design, whether or not its perforation teeth are intact, bent or missing; whether or not the stamp is creased, smudged, or damaged by tiny pinholes; the quality and quantity of gum on its back; and—if it is a used specimen—the degree to which the cancellation mark obscures the design.

In stamp advertisements, you will find that some dealers use very imprecise language. They will describe a stamp as "a gem," or "a beauty." Beware of such terminology.

Although there is a certain degree of subjectivity in grading the condition of a stamp, connoisseurs and reputable dealers usually adhere to very precise criteria and language.

There are six commonly accepted terms to describe a stamp's condition: *Superb* (S), *Very Fine* (VF), *Fine* (F), *Average* (Av. or Avg.), *Good* (G), *Poor* (P). Some nitpickers wedge *Extremely Fine or Extra Fine* (XF) in between Superb and Very Fine. Others put *Very Good* (VG) between Fine and Good, thus eliminating the Average designation. Some put *Fair* in between Good and Poor. But these are less frequently used.

WHAT'S ACCEPTABLE FOR INVESTORS

If you are an investor, your task is simplified. Don't accept anything less than Fine.

A Superb stamp is one that is perfect in every way, front and back, and its design is centered with mathematical precision.

A Very Fine stamp falls a bit short of this exacting standard, sometimes only because its centering is slightly off.

A Fine stamp may be Superb or Very Fine in every respect, but its design may be far off center. However, to qualify as Fine, its design must not be so far off that it touches the perforations.

The *Scott Catalogue* lists prices for stamps in Fine condition. Those in Very Fine or Superb condition often sell for above the catalogue price, sometimes *too* far above. In fact, some collectors get so carried away in their zeal to acquire a Superb stamp that they bid astronomical prices. If this pleases them, who can argue? But if they bought the stamp for purposes of investment, they could be in for a rude shock, because the next buyer may not be quite so enthused with this "gem."

If a stamp is Fine or Very Fine (some that are in between are described F-VF), and you needn't pay a large premium to acquire it, this is the kind of item that makes a sensible investment—provided it's the right stamp, of course. I strongly advise against paying large premiums, far in excess of catalogue value, until you have acquired sufficient experience to be convinced that the price level is supported by demand, and not by the whimsy of a handful of bid-happy collectors.

WHAT TO AVOID

If a stamp has a *tear* or a *fault,* forget it. If a stamp has a *thin,* meaning that some of the paper in front or back has been worn away, proceed with caution. The stamp is not technically intact, and doesn't rate as ideal investment material, unless the thin is tiny or negligible. Also forget stamps that have *broken perfs,* meaning that one or more of the perforation teeth are missing or damaged.

If a stamp has been *repaired,* meaning that a tear has been fixed or a missing perforation tooth replaced, it might possibly be worth acquiring at a bargain price, providing the work was done by an expert. But great caution is advisable. If a stamp has been *regummed,* this means that someone has added new gum to the back, in order to enhance its value. This stamp could be worth acquiring, but it is worth less than one that is never-hinged, or retains most of its original gum. A reliable dealer will not withhold information about repairs or regumming. He knows the score—even if you aren't able to spot the facts.

Later on, we'll explore the complex world of price differences based on condition. In the meantime, make sure that you are familiar with these basic terms. If you are, you now command the beginnings of stamp language.

ADDITIONAL SOURCES OF KNOWLEDGE

In the next few pages, I want to mention some of the myriad sources of knowledge about stamps.

If you are already a collector, but not yet an investor, many of these sources will be familiar to you. If this book is your introduction to philately, the following data will save you weeks and months of hunting.

Don't be cowed by the abundance of material. As time passes, you may well settle for reading a book or two on the subject, buying one catalogue, subscribing to one periodical, and perhaps joining one philatelic society or stamp club. But I do want to give you some idea of the abundance of options.

Many items can be borrowed from your public library, but be prepared to spend a little money on these materials. By investing $25 to $50 per year in the acquisition of stamp knowledge, you may well create opportunities to earn thousands in return. Also, as an investor in stamps, the money you spend on acquiring knowledge is tax deductible.

A FEW BASIC BOOKS

For starters, you can't go wrong spending a mere half dollar on *Stamp Collecting: Your Introduction to a Fascinating Hobby*, by Franklin R. Bruns (Washington Press, 1776 Springfield Ave., Maplewood, N.J. 07040). This forty-page booklet by the former curator of the National Postage Stamp Collection at the Smithsonian offers an excellent glossary of basic terms and a brief history of philately.

Also helpful is *Scott's New Handbook for Philatelics*. Published by Simon & Schuster of New York, it is a 192-page book that retails for $4.95. It includes a glossary of terms, a list of stamp societies, foreign exchange rates, and other useful information.

At your local Post Office, you can purchase *United States Stamps & Stories* ($2), a 224-page handbook that depicts most U.S. stamps in full color and shows their current catalogue value. This book also includes a glossary and other helpful background data.

Perhaps the greatest bargain of all is *United States Postage Stamps* published by the Philatelic Affairs Division of the U.S. Postal Service, Washington, D.C. 20260. This offers a treasure of information on U.S. stamps, including an appendix listing actual quantities of stamps printed. The 300 loose-leaf pages cover stamps up through 1942 and costs $4.70, with an extra $3.45 for a sturdy binder.

The collector/investor who specializes in rare U.S. stamps is strongly advised to acquire *The United States Stamps of the 19th Century* by L.G. Brookman. Published in three volumes, this has

900 pages of excellent information and 1,100 fine illustrations. It is available for $30 from the Brookman Company, 76 South Orange Ave., South Orange, N.J. 07079.

One of the most lavish introductory books on stamps I've ever seen is the recently published *Pictorial Treasury of U.S. Stamps,* which lists at $19.95 and is published by Collectors Institute, Ltd. 10102 "F" Street, Omaha, Nebraska 68127. This book reproduces over 1,250 stamps in their authentic colors, and provides a wealth of data, including a digest of market values, shown at ten-year intervals since 1925.

For pleasure, and knowledge, I recommend that you look for books by Herman Herst, Jr., a stamp dealer with many years of experience, and a sense of humor. The two that I've read are *Nassau Street: A Quarter Century of Stamp Dealing,* and *Fun and Profit in Stamp Collecting.* Both were published by Meredith Press of New York. Herst is a good storyteller, and many of his anecdotes contain useful advice about the pitfalls of investing without benefit of knowledge.

USEFUL PERIODICALS

The indispensable publication for any collector/investor is *Linn's Stamp News,* a weekly tabloid that costs 45 cents per copy and $6.50 per year (P.O. Box 29, Sidney, Ohio 45365). *Linn's* calls itself "the world's largest and most informative weekly stamp paper." This is true. A typical issue has close to 100 pages, packed with articles, retail price lists, auction offers, marketing trends, "buy" and "sell" ads, etc. An hour spent each week scanning the ads is an hour well spent. It is, in effect, the *Wall Street Journal* of philately.

Other worthwhile publications are:

- *Stamps,* a weekly magazine that costs $5 per year (153 Waverly Place, New York, N.Y. 10014).

- *Western Stamp Collector,* another tabloid, which costs $5.50 per year (P.O. Box 10, Albany, Oregon 97321).
- *Scott Monthly Journal* notes new Scott Catalogue entries and price changes; costs $7.50 per year (Scott Publications, 10102 "F" Street, Omaha, Nebraska 68127).
- *The American Philatelist,* a monthly magazine for specialists, received by members of the American Philatelic Society, who pay $7 annual dues (APS, Box 800, State College, Pa. 16801).
- *Stamp Wholesaler,* published twenty-one times a year, is excellent, if you can get it. Subscriptions are $7 (Box 529, Burlington, Vt. 05401). This magazine lists data on wholesale prices, marketing tips, prices realized at recent auctions, etc. It is normally available only to stamp dealers. However, since there is no formal licensing procedure for becoming a dealer, virtually anyone can qualify. For example, if you have a letterhead that identifies you as a seller of stamps, or a clipping of a newspaper classified ad where you have offered stamps for sale, you might be considered a part-time dealer, and can try requesting a subscription.
- *Publications Directory,* Vol. I, lists philatelic publications in the United States, including many that treat esoteric facets of the hobby. It retails for $3 (Stamps Information Associates, Inc., 675 Massachusetts Ave., Cambridge, Mass. 02139). Volumes II and III list publications in foreign countries and Great Britain, respectively.

CATALOGUES LISTING STAMP PRICES

The seminal sources of data on stamps and their value (particularly if you reside in the United States) are the *Scott's Standard Postage Stamp Catalogues,* which are divided into four separate volumes: Volume I covers the United States, United Nations and British Commonwealth; Volume II and Volume III cover the rest of the world; Volume IV is the *United States Specialized*, which treats stamps of this country in extensive detail.

It is *essential* that you become familiar with the *Scott Catalogues*. The introductory pages, containing "Information for Collectors," are most instructive. Volume I, which contains listings for all U.S. stamps, features detailed illustrations of each stamp. A value is assigned to every stamp, both in unused and used condition. *Scott's U.S. Specialized Catalogue* volume offers even more information, including values for such commonly traded items as blocks, plate blocks and covers, as well as values for used stamps with rare cancellations.

Scott Catalogues retail for $12 to $13 per volume but are usually available at discount, for as low as $8 apiece. By saving these catalogues, you will, over the years, accumulate an invaluable storehouse of marketing data. You can also find back issues at libraries and make xerox copies of relevant sections. Old volumes are sometimes offered for sale. I recently saw, for example, a classified ad that offered Scott catalogues dating as far back as 1909 (Rodman Borgstede, RFD #3, Plattsburgh, N.Y. 12091).

The *Scott Catalogues* are issued yearly. Volume I appears in the summer, and the *U.S. Specialized* comes out in December, often reflecting significant last-minute price revisions.

The publishers of *Scott Catalogues* do *not* sell stamps. Their publications are a guide to market prices, based on a consensus of many experts.

WHAT CATALOGUE PRICES REALLY MEAN

Now here is a vitally important *caveat* for collector/investors. As Scott itself warns, the catalogue value assigned is "for fine specimens when offered by an informed dealer to an informed buyer."

But this is not as simple or universal as it sounds. You will *rarely* pay the exact price mentioned by Scott for a given stamp. Some are available at enormous discounts from the Scott value; others sell for a substantial premium "above Scott." This may sound confusing, but in a subsequent chapter you will find a discussion that clarifies the issue of stamp pricing.

In conjunction with the Scott publications, one should be familiar with other catalogues, some of which are produced by companies that *do* sell stamps, and whose quotations are the actual prices charged for the items they have in stock, although you can always bargain for, and sometimes get, a discount.

The best known of these "sale price" catalogues are:

- *Harris Stamps of the United States, United Nations, Canada and Provinces,* available at many stores for $1.50 (published by H.E. Harris & Co., Inc., Boston, Mass. 02117). This is the Harris Company's retail price list for single stamps, plate books, mint sheets, etc. It is profusely illustrated. Many local retailers will use the Harris catalogue as their own, offering you stamps at the prices listed, or at a discount.

- *Stamps of the United States* is a 138-page, pocket-size price list, published for retail stamp dealers by the Brookman Company, and sold retail for 75 cents. This identifies stamps by Scott number and has prices for Fine and Average specimens, both used and unused. In this case, the Brookman Company itself does not sell stamps at retail, and the prices are meant to be charged by the retailers who purchase this catalogue. Some retailers will offer you a discount from the Brookman price.

Also useful is the price list of *U.S., U.S. Possessions, Hawaii, Philippine Islands and British North America,* issued quarterly at $3 per year by Stanley Gibbons, Inc. (38 Park Row, New York, N.Y. 10038). Regular "active" customers receive it free.

The Minkus Company is involved in the publication of catalogues and albums, and in the sale of stamps largely through retail store outlets, such as Gimbels in New York City. Its *New American Stamp Catalog* utilizes what is known as the "Minkus numbering system." However, for the convenience of its customers, Minkus' retail price lists include both the Scott and Minkus numbers to identify each stamp.

If you decide to move into some specialized area of philatelic investment, one of the following catalogues may prove valuable:

- For airmail stamps, United States and otherwise, the "bible" is the *Sanabria World Airmail Catalogue,* which comes in two volumes and is expensive (about $75). Check with Collectors National Stamp Service, 139 Rockaway Avenue, Suite Six, Weymouth, Mass. 02188.

- In the field of first day covers, there is much information in *U.S. Classic Cachets, 1923-1933.* This 150-page catalogue offers detailed descriptions of 1,375 known classic cachets (first day covers) and is available for $3.50 from Professor Earl Planty, 3602 N.W. 84th Ave., Coral Springs, Fla. 33065. Also helpful is the *U.S. Specialized Catalog of First Day Covers,* 100 pages, $1.25, from Washington Press, 1776 Springfield Ave., Maplewood, N.J. 07040.

- Collectors of plate number blocks will want to refer to the *Durland Plate Book Catalogue,* which costs $4.50 and is available at some retailers. Those who collect plate number single stamps will be interested in *Hebert's Catalogue of Used Plate Number Singles,* which costs $4 and is available from George Shapiro of Trans-Pacific Stamp Company, Box 48715, Los Angeles, Cal. 90048. This volume begins with plate number singles of the 1893 Columbians, and includes prices by number and position, with prices also for "ZIP" and "Mail Early" singles.

- Postal history also holds great potential for investors, but requires specialized knowledge. The most authoritative source in this area is the series of volumes published by

Higgins & Gage, Inc., 23 No. Altadena Drive, Pasadena, Cal. 91107. Each volume of this scholarly series treats a couple of countries at a time. Write to them for a description of the material they have published on U.S. postal history.

SPECIAL SOURCES FOR FOREIGN STAMPS

Although the *Scott Catalogues* and others published in the United States offer prices for all nations of the world, they are of limited value if you invest in stamps from abroad. Stamp collectors are chauvinistic. Many countries have catalogues of their own, in which their own stamps are described in rich detail, and market values may be pegged considerably higher.

If you specialize in European stamps, for example, it could be suicidal to depend exclusively upon the *Scott Catalogues* and to ignore those published by Gibbons, Michel and Yvert, which are fare more authoritative and assign more realistic market values. Virtually every nation from Australia to Venezuela has a locally published catalogue that is essential to the specialist.

SOCIETIES AND CLUBS

Philately can be a solitary avocation with all dealings carried out by mail. But if you are the gregarious type, it provides all manner of social activities. There are numerous advantages to at least limited participation in some type of group. You can learn a great deal from fellow club members, and you can frequently buy, sell, or trade stamps through such organizations.

As for the social aspect, philatelists represent a stimulating cross-section of our society. A recently published list of new members in a major stamp society included a bus driver from

Seattle, a TV engineer from Miami, a university professor from Toronto, a retired Army officer from Chicago, a homicide detective from Houston, an FBI agent from San Francisco, the president of a vacuum cleaner company from a small town in New York State, a minister from Buffalo, a geophysicist from Silver Spring, Maryland, and a stockbroker from Fresno, California. As for gender, the majority of collectors are men, but there are many thousands of women philatelists, and more than a few husband-wife teams.

For stamp clubs in your area, consult your local newspaper. *Linn's Stamp News*, which maintains a register of clubs worldwide, lists 1,348 in the United States and 331 abroad. This is just a fraction of the actual number. If you live in New York, for example, you'll find 150 stamp clubs in that state alone. Even North Dakota has 2, and most states have 10 or more. To locate clubs in your area, write to Linn's Club Center, Box 29, Sidney, Ohio 45365.

You should belong to at least one national stamp society. I believe the one most beneficial to U.S. collectors is the American Philatelic Society (APS), PO Box 800, State College, Pa. 16801. For an admission fee of $3 and $7 annual dues, you receive multiple benefits.

The APS has more than 30,000 members in fifty states and eighty-eight foreign countries. It publishes a 100-page monthly magazine, *The American Philatelist*, which features informative articles, advertisements and news of new issues. The APS Sales Division will, upon request, mail "circuits" of stamps for sale by members. About $1.5 million worth of members' stamps are sold each year in these "circuits." It's a fine way to buy—and to sell your surplus holdings. For this service, the APS takes a 20 percent commission on sales.

APS members can also buy "all risk" insurance for their stamp collections. The APS Expert Committee will, for a fee, render an opinion about the identity or genuineness of your rare stamps. Also, the APS has a research library where you can borrow books or get photo copies of reference materials. Before accepting you as a member, the APS will make a careful check of your references; membership in this society therefore constitutes an informal type of "credit reference" that will be helpful when you purchase stamps elsewhere.

The Philatelic Foundation, 99 Park Avenue, New York, N.Y. 10016 is a non-profit organization chartered by the State University of New York for philatelic study and research. Membership ranges from $10 for subscriber status and runs up to $1,000 or more for benefactors. The Foundation has an excellent research library. Its most essential service is the identification of stamp forgeries. For a fee, it will "expertize" stamps and issue a certificate. Also, it issues bulletins about stamp forgeries. (See more about this in the chapter titled "Fakes and Forgeries.")

I think that memberships in the APS and the Philatelic Foundation are essential for any serious collector/investor. Here are a few other organizations that may prove worth looking into.

- Similar to, but smaller than, the APS is the Society of Philatelic Americans (SPA), which also publishes a monthly journal, a sample of which you can get for 50 cents. Contact SPA, Dept. S, Box 42060, Cincinnati, Ohio 45242.
- The U.S. Philatelic Classics Society also publishes a journal. For membership, write to Melvin W. Schuk, 6 Laconia Road, Worcester, Mass. 01609. For sample copies of the journal, called *The Chronicle of U.S. Classic Postal Issues,* write to Box 2424, Arlington, Va. 22202.
- The Bureau Issues Association publishes the monthly *United States Specialist.* Write to executive secretary Esther H. Sullivan (19 Maple St., Arlington, Mass. 02174).
- The American Plate Number Single Society, which

examines its particular specialty in U.S. stamps, can be contacted at 10926 Annette Ave., Tampa, Fla. 33612.

• The American Philatelic Research Library, Box 338-S, State College, Pa. 16801 publishes a quarterly *Philatelic Literature Review*. A sample copy is 50 cents. Annual membership of $3 includes a subscription to the review.

If you become active in the buying and selling of stamps, you might check with the American Stamp Dealers Association, 595 Madison Avenue, New York, N.Y. 10022, to see whether membership in that organization would be beneficial to you.

If your collecting interests reach beyond the borders of the United States, there are numerous groups that may appeal to you.

The National Philatelic Society of England, 44 Fleet St., London E.C. 4, England, issues a bimonthly journal, *The Stamp Lover*. The British-American Collectors Club, 9 Victoria Close, Worsley, Manchester, M28 4HG, England, has philatelic contacts for its members in thirty English-speaking countries. If you send them a 10-cent stamp you will get a quick airmail reply from them about their services.

The France & Colonies Philatelic Society issues a quarterly journal at 50 cents for a sample. Contact Eric Spiegel, 300 W. 109th St., New York, N.Y. 10025.

Specialists in Israel will want to investigate the Society of Israel Philatelists, which publishes a journal. Write to Dr. A. Friedberg, 31715 Vine St., Willowick, Ohio 44094. Also, check out the Eilat Club, Box 542, Eilat, Israel, which can sell you new stamp and coin issues.

Or how about the Portugal & Colonies Philatelic Society? For a sample copy of their quarterly journal, contact the society secretary, Nancy M. Gaylord, 43 Dundee Road, Stamford, Conn. 06903.

If your tastes run to Cuban stamps, send 25 cents for a sample issue of the *Cuban Philatelist* to Laura G. Cantens, Box

45-0055, Miami, Fla. 33145. The Cuban Philatelic Society of America holds regular meetings in Miami and New York.

The list of clubs and societies can fill a book. I have risked going on at some length to indicate to you the rich possibilities of becoming expert in some specialized area of philately.

As I said earlier, "Knowledge is power." Each time a stamp collector/investor buys or sells, he pits his knowledge (or ignorance) against the person at the other end of the transaction. If you've ever visited a used car lot, you'll know what I mean. Just "kicking the tires" isn't enough. The next chapter will discuss the kinds of stamps most likely to appreciate in value from year to year.

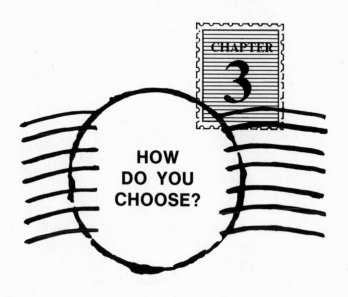

CHAPTER 3

HOW DO YOU CHOOSE?

Back in October 1886, an article in the quarterly journal *The California Collector* lamented:

> It is now only forty-five years since the first postage stamp was issued in England, and yet we find ourselves in a labyrinth of stamps, coming from here and there, each month the complication grows larger and stronger.

Noting that more than 30,000 stamps had already been issued, the writer predicted that "by the year 2085" there could be as many as 107,000 different varieties of stamps on the market. He was, it turns out, quite conservative in his prediction. You can already buy mounted collections of 125,000 different worldwide stamps, and thousands of new stamps are issued each year by hundreds of nations around the globe.

The hard truth is that few of these rise appreciably in value. The United States, for example, has issued close to 2,000 regular and airmail stamps since 1847, but only about 100 of them, on the basis of past performance, rate as good growth properties. How does one choose the good performers?

A few basic principles can help you decide in which country's stamps to invest, and which few of that country's issues represent an investment, not a gamble.

SEVEN BASIC RULES FOR CANNY INVESTORS

1. The beauty of a stamp's color or design has little to do with its investment value—the world's most valuable stamp is a faded, tatty bit of paper. As with most commodities, a stamp's value is based on supply and demand. It must be scarce, but scarcity is *not* enough. It must also be wanted.

Herman Herst, Jr., has a story that illustrates this point quite tellingly. Some years ago, Arthur Hind of Utica, New York, was the proud possessor of the faded, tatty stamp I just mentioned: the unique 1-cent British Guiana stamp of 1856, which then had a catalogue value of $35,000 (it is now up to $325,000). An Austrian collector, Philippe von Ferrary, wrote to Hind and suggested an even swap. The Austrian also had a unique stamp, from the Indian feudatory state of Poonch. Hind refused. Some years later, the Poonch stamp was purchased at auction for $1,200. It, too, was unique, but for some inexplicable reason it was not as "wanted." Exactly why some scarce stamps are more wanted than others defies a simple formula. But by the end of this chapter you will, perhaps, develop an instinct for making educated guesses.

2. All stamp-issuing nations have at least a few good investment items, but certain nations are, in general, "better" than others—philatelically speaking, of course.

3. A stamp's basic demand is generated in its home country. To collect stamps is, in a sense, to collect history. Strong local stamp markets exist in those nations that have a large, literate middle class. In these nations you will find large populations who have the interest, the capital, and the leisure time to become involved in stamps. When no internal demand exists for a nation's stamps, they are usually so plentiful that supplies rarely become scarce, and values do not climb steadily.

4. Older stamps—those of the nineteenth century and of the very early twentieth century—are, as a rule, better investments than recent issues. These older stamps have had time to become naturally scarce. Since the 1920s, the increased use of the mails and growing worldwide interest in stamp collecting have caused post offices to issue very large quantities of stamps. You may find that some of these recent stamps have very high prices, but their true value is quite shaky. With recent stamps, it is possible for a single large dealer or a consortium of dealers to corner the market on a single item, buying up a major share of the entire issue, and then inflate the asking price.

A recent 50-cent stamp of Jamaica, for example, was issued in a quantity of only 83,000. For an investment of slightly over $40,000 a dealer could theoretically buy up the entire supply. He could charge outrageous prices to collectors who are eager to fill empty album spaces. But, if a collector decided to sell the stamp back to him, the dealer's buy-price would be quite low, since he would have thousands of this item on hand.

While it is unlikely that any dealer would try to buy up an entire issue of a new stamp, the dealer could easily purchase enough of them to create false scarcities. This is impossible with high-priced stamps issued fifty years ago or more. There may have been attempts to corner the market at that time, but by now no single dealer, even if he were alive, could resist the pressure to sell off his stock at a profit.

The plain fact is: Most of the good nineteenth- and early

twentieth-century material is in the hands of individual collectors, in limited quantities. They are available, but no one controls their supply. In fact, dealers compete with collectors in efforts to purchase them, in order to replenish their inventories. They are naturally scarce.

This is why I regard as suspect all brand-new but so-called "limited editions" of anything, be it stamps, coins, or silver commemorative medals. You may get some ingenuous collector to pay you a premium price for your holdings, but dealers won't.

For example, I recently called a major dealer in commemorative silver medals to ascertain his buy-price for a set issued a few years ago by The Franklin Mint. The original sales price of these silver medals was approximately $1,600. The dealer offered to buy them for $900! Even had he offered the original value of $1,600 this would have represented a loss to the investor, because of the inflation of the past few years.

5. Stamps do *not* always rise in value. But, as I have said before, unlike the stock market, stamps rise and fall gradually, on a year-to-year basis. Also unlike the stock market, stamps that have a long history of rising in value, tend to continue doing so. They did even during the Depression of the 1930s.

6. As a rule, unused stamps tend to grow more rapidly in value than used stamps. There are exceptions. For example, residents of some remote countries write relatively few letters, so it is easier to find an unused stamp than one that was cancelled in the mails. This is why a wholesaler who recently offered stamps of certain former British colonies was charging a 20 percent premium for used stamps. But for starters, stick to unused stamps.

7. Very frequently, a good investment item that reaches a high bracket of market value, say $1,000 or more, will continue to increase in value, but at a slower pace. This occurs because the number of collectors who can afford this stamp has been thinned out; its mass market disappears and the stamp begins to exchange hands among a smaller group of affluent collectors. On the other hand, more moderately priced stamps, between fifty and a few

hundred dollars, are within the reach of the mass market. And, providing they are relatively scarce, they tend to appreciate in value at a more rapid rate.

BE WARY OF NEW ISSUES

Knowing all of this is helpful, but it still doesn't answer the question: Which stamps are good investments?

The first part of the answer is: *Be wary of new and recently issued stamps.* Yes, I know there are exceptions. A major dealer in new issues points out, and truthfully so, that over the years he has supplied clients with many fine investment values. I'll cite a few:

	Cost per Stamp at Time of Issue	1975 Catalogue Value
1956 Cambodia (Scott No. 53-53)	$ 2.95	$ 30.00
1960 Cyprus (Scott No. 183-197)	8.95	103.00
1966 Rhodesia (Scott No. 222).	3.00	25.00
1967 Cook Islands (Scott No. 192-194).	39.50	650.00
1971 Pitcairn Islands (Scott No. 118).	.20	5.50

But these few winners were issued along with hundreds of other new stamps that have not gone up appreciably in value. To purchase all of them would have cost you a small fortune. It is impossible to chart the investment future of a new or recently issued stamp. All the principles mentioned above are merely guidelines for a stamp's upward rise, and the importance of each factor is hard to gauge.

Guessing the future of stamps that have no past is gambling, not investment. Some new stamps simply never rise in value, except for tiny increments that reflect inflationary pressures. Others enjoy an early spurt of popularity because of some fad, or due to heavy stamp dealer advertising. Then, because supplies of the stamp are abundant, they subside in value, never to rise again. Yes, if you buy every new issue that appears, you will surely find a few that multiply in value. But you will have hundreds (or thousands) of others that will stand still, resulting in a loss. By this scattershot method, you will only have one, or a few, of the winners. Isn't it more sensible to invest all of your venture capital in a few winners? To do so, you have to wait and see which few stamps are breaking away from the huge pack of new issues. It can take thirty years, sometimes, before a stamp's market value is solidly established.

A perfect example is the case of the $5 Columbian of 1893, which I mentioned briefly before. When this was first issued, many collectors howled that it was an overpriced, unnecessary stamp and was being sold by the post office merely to derive revenues from collectors. Thirty-two years later, in 1925, the market value of this $5 stamp was only $10. But by then, the original protests had long been forgotten. A new generation of collectors realized that this was the key stamp in a popular set. You couldn't own a complete set without it. And, above all, it was *scarce*. Only 27,350 copies had been issued by the post office, and the number of interested collectors was far larger.

By 1935, the stamp had more than doubled in value, and its worth continued to multiply with each succeeding decade. Its present catalogue value is $900, and it grows at a healthy pace each year.

LOOK FOR THE TRACK RECORD

That is why sensible investors focus almost exclusively on older stamps, which have a long track record, or what I prefer to call a clear "upward trajectory." The answer, then, is: Don't try to predict which stamps will go up in value. And don't pay attention to tipsters who predict that this or that stamp "will likely go up" or is "way underpriced" or was issued in "such small quantities" that it is "bound" to go up. This type of conjecture has gone on for years and is rarely accurate. Furthermore, in a few cases, the so-called tipster may have a large stock of these stamps that he wishes to sell. Instead, identify those stamps that *are rising now, and have been doing so for many years.* Finding these involves what I call an "ever-narrowing search."

The first step is to eliminate those stamps that have little or no investment potential. Choose a country that interests you. Let's say Canada (not a bad investment, by the way). Buy or borrow the *Scott Catalogues* for this year, five years ago and ten years ago. On a sheet of ruled paper, write down the name of the country and the following headings, as in the example below:

CANADA

Catalogue value:

Catalogue No.	10 yrs.	5 yrs.	Today

Now, refer to this year's *Scott Catalogue* and the edition of ten years ago. Begin with stamp number one of the country you're checking. Look up its value today, for an unused single copy, and its value ten years ago.

Suppose that the first stamp you compare was catalogued at $20 in 1965 and today (1975) is valued at $35. This $15 rise in catalogue value seems impressive, but remember that it took ten years to increase that much. How much has the value of the dollar decreased during the same time? How much would $20 have grown in a savings account over a ten-year period?

Considering these factors, you'll quickly realize that a $15 increase, 75 percent over ten years, is not altogether impressive. Of course, it's better than the performance of many stocks and mutual funds that have gone down in value over ten years' time, but other stamps have done much better than the hypothetical item we have just examined.

HOW TO CALCULATE A WORTHWHILE RETURN

A stamp that appreciates at the rate of 10 percent yearly will be worth about one and one-half times its original value by the fifth year, and two and one-half times its original value by the tenth year.

A stamp that appreciates at the rate of 12 percent a year will triple in value by the tenth year. A stamp gaining at a 15 percent yearly rate will double by the fifth year and quadruple by the tenth year. One that appreciates 20 percent yearly will sextuple in ten years.

The following chart will be useful. It shows the approximate increases, year by year, for $100 invested at various rates of return, based on compound interest.

Year	10%	12%	15%	20%
1	110.	112.	115.	120.
2	121.	125.	132.	144.
3	132.	140.	152.	172.
4	145.	157.	174.	207.
5	160.	175.	201.	248.
6	176.	196.	231.	298.
7	193.	219.	265.	358.
8	213.	245.	305.	429.
9	234.	274.	351.	515.
10	257.	307.	404.	619.

When cross-checking catalogues of previous years, the above chart will help you determine whether or not a stamp is appreciating at a rate that would qualify it as an attractive investment.

USING CATALOGUE PRICE AS A BAROMETER

Before going any further, let's briefly discuss the question of catalogue value. As you will soon learn, if a Fine unused stamp was catalogued at $100 ten years ago, that doesn't mean that it was selling for $100. By the same token, if you discover that the same stamp is worth $400 in today's catalogue, this doesn't mean that it always sells for $400. In both cases, the stamp may have been available for a substantial discount from the catalogue price. Or, it may sell at a premium far above catalogue value. But don't let this concern you yet.

The important thing to remember now is that a stamp's catalogue value is a faithful barometer of its actual market value. If the catalogue value has tripled in the past ten years, *it is most likely that the market value has tripled also.*

In perhaps half an hour, you can cross-check the catalogue values of an entire country's stamps. You'll find that only a handful have appreciated at least 10 percent a year for the past decade. Show no mercy. You may find a stamp that was worth $50 ten years ago, and has risen to $100 today. This looks attractive. But you might have done almost as well, without risk, in a savings bank. Forget it. Drop it from your list. Many of the stamps from a given country will have stood still in the past ten years, a few will have gone down slightly, and others will have appreciated only as a result of inflation. The potential "blue chips" will have gone up at least two and one-half times.

There are enough of these; don't waste time with the others. List the good ones, as I've suggested, including their catalogue values today and ten years ago.

Now for the next step. Some stamps show uneven growth patterns and should be weeded out. They may have jumped sensationally in value just once during the past decade (perhaps eight years ago) and stood still ever since. Or, they may have suddenly exploded last year, after a long hiatus. These stamps are suspect. They may be going up due to speculation by dealers, rather than solid market demand.

You can begin to weed these out by looking at your five-year-old catalogue. Remember now, we are only looking at a few stamps, those that have gone up by at least two and one-half times in the past decade. But we want to check their steadiness.

HOW TO CHECK FOR STEADY APPRECIATION

1. If a stamp was worth $100 a decade ago, and if it maintains a 10 percent annual growth rate, it should have been worth about $160 by the fifth year.
2. A 12 percent annual rate means that a $100 stamp ten years ago would have grown to $175 by the fifth year.
3. A 15 percent annual growth rate means that a stamp worth $100 ten years ago would have appreciated to $201 by the fifth year.
4. A 20 percent growth rate means that, by the fifth year, a $100 stamp would be catalogued at $248.

By performing this five-year test, you will weed out some of those apparent "blue chips" from your list. Remember again: We are looking for steady growth. Ten years is a fair test of time, and there is no reason why a truly good stamp should not appreciate in value during both halves of the decade. In the case of some countries, this method will pare your list down to just a dozen or so stamps. These are the ones with serious potential.

HOW TO BUILD A "PRICE PORTRAIT"

List each of the serious candidates on a separate index card. Here's how I do it:

Canada	
Cat. No. 65	$5 olive-green of 1897
1965	$100.
1970	$225.
1975	$425.

Now we're getting somewhere. We are beginning to build a "price portrait" of a stamp with serious investment potential. In the example I have just cited, we have a $5 olive-green Canadian stamp of 1897, with a *Scott Catalogue* number of 65. In 1965, it was valued at $100. Five years later, it rose to $225. Ten years later, it was up to $425. This stamp has been appreciating steadily at a rate of more than 15 percent a year. It looks quite promising, but I still wouldn't reach for my checkbook.

Someone once said that genius was "one part inspiration and 99 percent perspiration." Before investing any of your money, I urge you to invest a bit more time. Sound investment seeks maximum gain with minimum risk. Let's reduce that risk some more.

Before acquiring Canada #65, let's check its catalogue value over the past three years. If a stamp hasn't moved up in value during the past three years of furious philatelic investment, something is wrong. Check it out.

If it passes this test, did it do as well during the bullish stock market of the late 1960s as it's done during the bearish period of the 1970s? Do a little more research. Look back ten, twenty, thirty years ago (old catalogues may be available at your library). Has the stamp been following a steady upward trajectory?

HOW RESEARCH PAYS OFF BIG

It certainly has. I located a 1937 *Scott Catalogue* and found that this Canadian stamp (now valued at $425) was then priced at only $18.50. I also consulted a 1964 *Scott Catalogue* and saw it valued at $90, meaning that it jumped more than 11 percent the following year. In 1969, it was valued at $200, and jumped by $25 (12.5 percent) the next year. By 1972, it was up to $300, and two years later had climbed to $350. And between 1974 and 1975, it appreciated by 21 percent, easily outpacing inflation, and leaving stocks and mutual funds in the dust.

If purchased at the right price—and in the proper condition—I am confident that this stamp has far better investment potential than all the "hot issues" touted by Wall Street specialists.

You already know that stamps are not like stocks. You can, of course, chart the movement of stocks, but only over relatively short periods of time, and the trick with stocks is not to chart growth, but to understand cyclical movement. Companies merge, or disappear. But you will find that what was a good stamp ten or twenty years ago is very likely to be a good stamp today. I have yet to find a truly scarce older stamp that has dropped in value over the long term.

By using the criteria of the past, you will narrow your list of "blue chips" down to a very small number. Now, let's look at what to do about your list today.

If you're going to buy the stamp, you don't want to pay an absurdly high price for it. I would want to know the stamp's current wholesale and retail price and its prevalent value at auction too. Is the stamp frequently listed in dealer "buy" ads? This is a good sign that it continues to be in strong demand. Then, and only then, would I consider investing.

This may sound like a rather arduous, time-consuming process to go through merely to identify a few stamps that have investment potential. But, remember, it's your money. Furthermore, the research you carry out now is likely to hold true for several years. *A good stamp remains good.*

How to purchase these stamps—and for what price—will be discussed in a subsequent chapter. Let's continue now with what to consider buying.

THE CASE FOR INVESTING IN UNUSED SINGLES

You'll notice that I've asked you to compare the values of the unused single stamps of Canada. Unused singles are the most commonly traded type of stamps. Their values are frequently publicized in ads, auctions and catalogues.

As you become more advanced in philately, you may wish to explore the investment potential of plate number blocks, mint sheets, coil pairs, even postal stationery, stampless covers, or rare first day covers. All of these specialty areas can be profitable. But they require expertise. For the moment, let's keep it simple. Let's stick to unused singles.

You can try the ten-year comparison technique with every country in the world. They are all listed in the *Scott Catalogues.* But such a process is time-consuming. Some countries are known to be better than others for the reasons that I outlined earlier in this chapter.

THE FOUR FAVORED AREAS

Among the better countries are:

1. The United States, Canada and, to a lesser extent, the United Nations.

2. Great Britain and some of its former colonies, which are now members of the British Commonwealth.

3. Most nations of Western Europe, including the "extinct" nations and city-states of the nineteenth century.

4. Those nations in the rest of the world that operate on modern western-style economies: Japan, Taiwan, Israel, for example.

I should caution you again that this does not mean that all stamps of the better nations are good investments. For example, you can still buy full sheets of some U.S. stamps that were issued thirty years ago, at *below* their original face value!

Why? Let's take the case of the 3-cent Texas Centennial stamp of 1936 (Scott No. 776). The post office issued 124,000,000 of these. At the time, many naive Americans, convinced that they'd discovered a sure path to riches, bought them up by the sheet and stored them away. Of course, this created a temporary scarcity, but many of the guileless collectors soon tried to cash in, glutting the market with these stamps.

HOW TO ELIMINATE THE "NOT WANTED"

You can get a good feel for such a development by requesting the "buy" list of a major stamp company, such as H.E. Harris. In its 1975 booklet of *Top Buying Prices,* Harris lists the prices it will pay "per 100" for used and unused U.S. stamps. Look for that 1936 Texas Centennial stamp and you'll find a "NW" (Not Wanted) under the unused column. Harris doesn't want any. It probably has hundreds of mint sheets stored away. As for used copies, they will pay 48 cents per hundred, less than half a cent per stamp.

Starting with the 1930s, there are relatively few U.S. stamps that don't have a "NW" next to them in the Harris booklet. There are only a few exceptions.

Let's consider the 1943 5-cent Luxembourg stamp of the U.S. Overrun Countries series (Scott No. 912). Harris will pay you $5.10 per 100 unused copies. The face value is five cents. If you bought this stamp in 1943, and sold it to Harris today, you will have "profited" one-tenth of a cent per stamp—after thirty-two years! The lesson is clear, I hope. There are many, many U.S. stamps that are dirt cheap, decades after their issue. They are so common, in fact, that stamp dealers and auction galleries still use them for postage.

As you'll notice, I have excluded from my list the nations of Africa, Latin America, Asia, the Middle East and Eastern Europe. This doesn't mean that you won't find gems among their issues, particularly from the nineteenth century. But great caution is advisable.

FOUR GUIDELINES TO TRUE COST

To give you some idea of the relative strength of certain countries, let me cite some information from ads frequently placed in stamp journals by Edward Berman, a veteran retailer from Long Island, who has a mailing list of 3,000 clients. Berman mails to his clients album sheets with stamps from all nations, and the following guidelines:

1. Most of his U.S. stamps cost about 50 percent of the *Scott Catalogue* value.

2. Stamps of Great Britain and British Colonies also sell for about 50 percent of the *Scott Catalogue* price.

3. Stamps of Scandinavia, France, Italy, Germany and their colonies sell for about 40 percent of Scott.

4. Issues from other parts of Europe and Africa, Asia, South and Central America are sold for as little as 33⅓ percent of *Scott Catalogue*.

There are exceptions—particularly for rarities in certain countries, which sometimes sell for far above the catalogue price—but this shows you one veteran's perception of the stamp world. Mine is a rather conservative approach to stamp investment. Other stamp advisers will point out, and rightly so, that certain stamps from a few emerging nations are now beginning to take off. Ghana is one example. But in the world of stamps, a good investment will continue to be good for many years. Rather than gamble on those stamps that are likely to go up in value or are even beginning to go up, I believe that it is wiser to wait until they establish a clear pattern, and then invest in them as they continue to ascend. Once they begin a clear upward trajectory for a decade or more, they will continue to do so, no matter when you buy into them. This is what I define as investment, as opposed to gambling.

But enough theorizing for now. In the next chapter we'll identify some specific stamps of the United States that I regard as sound investments.

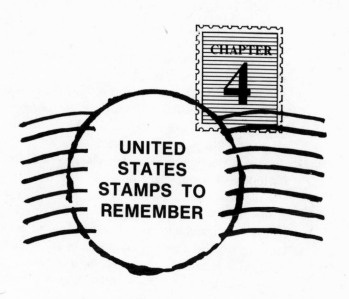

CHAPTER

4

**UNITED
STATES
STAMPS TO
REMEMBER**

If you'll recall Rule No. 3 in the previous chapter—a stamp's basic demand is generated in its home country—you will see why I believe that the safest choices for the new collector/investor are stamps of the United States, assuming that you are a U.S. resident.

It is here in the United States where you will likely buy your stamps, and also here where you, or your heirs, will probably dispose of them years hence.

According to a recent survey by the U.S. Postal Service, about 16 million people in this country collect stamps. Although many of them have interests in the stamps of other nations, about *97 percent* collect U.S. commemoratives. So you have a huge market.

Furthermore, one can spend a lifetime studying the stamps

of a single country, and the issues of the United States are numerous and complex enough to keep you more than occupied.

Where does one start in this vast field of choice? As of 1975, the United States had issued well over 2,000 different stamps. Not all of them, as I have shown, are good investments by any means—far from it.

I recall reading about a man who played the stock market in the following manner. He would take *The New York Times,* open it to the stock market quotations, and then blindly stab his pencil at the page. Wherever it fell, that was his choice. He gambled only a small amount in this way. Then he invested similar amounts on the advice of a stockbroker. After five years of nationwide economic prosperity, he had made a little money both ways. But there was not much difference between the relative performance of both groups of stocks.

One could try the same blind method with stamps, but there are far less arbitrary means of choosing winners.

A REVEALING COMPUTERIZED STUDY

An Illinois firm (Mardis Industries International of Bement, Illinois) in 1970 made a computerized study of 2,117 different U.S. postage stamps issued prior to 1940. The study traced their fluctuations in catalogue value during two periods: 1949–1969 and 1964–1969.

In a twenty-year period, these 2,117 items increased in value on an average of 5 percent a year, about the same as bank savings. However, over the shorter haul, the rise in value was 10.5 percent, about double the rate for bank savings. Stamps issued prior to 1900 had gone up by 13 percent and airmail stamps had gone up by nearly 11 percent.

Some items do even better. The computer survey included hundreds of common stamps, available at pennies apiece, that are disdained by knowledgeable collectors and investors. Some of the choicer items in this category rose at an average of 15 percent to 20 percent yearly.

In the main, the better U.S. investments are the U.S. classics, those issued from 1847 until 1900. Next are those from the middle period, between 1900 and 1930 (some people stretch this period up until 1940). Anything after that is a modern stamp, and, in my mind, is far less desirable for investment. To give you some idea why, you should know that the volume of U.S. mail is growing at about 2 percent yearly. Soon, mail volume will approach 100 *billion* pieces a year, including 63 billion letters.

"I don't buy modern issues myself for investment," says Greg Manning, one of the nation's largest stamp dealers. He regards speculation in sheets of modern stamps, and modern plate blocks, as "not very healthy." He will, of course, sell these items to anyone who desires them, but these are not the kind of stamps that go into Manning's personal vault for long-term appreciation.

SCARCITY COUNTS MOST

Among the few modern stamps that are attractive for investment, Manning believes, are plate blocks of $5 stamps.

These, he reasons, are issued in relatively small amounts. Also, it requires an investment of at least $20 to acquire a $5 plate block, which limits the number of collectors who can afford such an item. In years to come, therefore, it is likely that $5 plate blocks will be scarce. But, in general, Manning recommends "older issues with a track record."

The best items are the classics, not only because they are truly scarce, but because they are in strong demand. In the United States alone, as I said before, there are up to 16 million collectors. Let's write off the vast majority as amateurs and focus on the 1 million who collect on a serious basis. On second thought, let's narrow down even more sharply and zero in on the

100,000-plus persons who subscribe to the major stamp journals. These might be regarded as the hard-core serious market. Given this figure, what kind of true demand can exist for a stamp that was issued in quantities of 100 million or more? On the other hand, you can well imagine the competitive bidding for some of the classics, which were issued more than half a century ago in quantities of 20,000 and many of which have been lost, damaged or destroyed.

THE LIST OF 100 "BLUE CHIPS"

You can determine which of the U.S. stamps have the greatest investment potential by charting their upward trajectory, just as we did with the stamps of Canada in the previous chapter. Again, you do this with the *Scott Catalogue.*

I have charted the catalogue values of all unused U.S. single stamps, and tracked their percentage gain in value going back ten years, five years, and for the past three years. I eliminated all but about 100 of the 1,700-plus definitive, commemorative and air-mail stamps. I narrowed down this vast field of choice to select those few that have appreciated by an average of 12 percent or more per year, over a decade's time, during both bull and bear periods of the stock market, in times of boom and recession.

No system is perfect. No system can guarantee what will happen in the future. But these 100-odd U.S. stamps have demonstrated a clear upward trajectory that indicates stable growth in the years to come.

These are the ones that I'll invest in, providing I can acquire them in the proper condition, and at the proper price (see Chapter Six).

Before I give you the actual list of stamps that I recommend, let's explore another factor that affects a stamp's investment potential. It's commonly known as the concept of the "key stamp."

HOW TO SPOT KEY STAMPS

In 1907, the U.S. Post Office issued three stamps to commemorate the Jamestown Exposition held at Hampton Roads, Virginia. These three stamps are commonly known as the Jamestown Set. Their *Scott Catalogue* numbers are 328, 329 and 330. The latter one, known as the "high value" of the set, is the key stamp. Why? It's a simple question of arithmetic—the same law of supply and demand that I cited in connection with the $5 Columbian.

The table below shows how many of each stamp were issued by the post office, and the catalogue value of each, ten years ago and today:

Description/Scott No.	Quantity issued by post office	1965 cat. value	1975 cat. value
1c green (#328)	77,728,794	$1.85	$5.50
2c carmine (#329)	149,497,994	2.25	7.00
5c blue (#330)	7,980,594	16.00	40.00

As you can see, the post office issued these stamps in very different quantities. The idea was for the supply to reflect the projected demand for postal use. Human nature dictates that all serious collectors would strive to own the complete set of three stamps. But this is obviously impossible since the 1-cent is available in a quantity of 77 million; the 2-cent in an amount of 149 million; but the 5-cent only in less than 8 million.

This is precisely why the 1-cent stamp is available today for about 550 times its original post office value; the 2-cent can be purchased for 350 times its face value; but the 5-cent costs about *800 times* its original value!

By modern standards—when commemoratives are printed in amounts of 150 million—a stamp with an issue of under 8 million is relatively scarce. So the first two stamps of the Jamestown Set are relatively abundant. Virtually every collector of U.S. stamps has the first two. It is the natural drive to complete the set with the key 5-cent value that pushes its market price up to $40 and beyond, making it a fairly attractive investment item.

In fact, I would venture one step further. If the 1-cent and 2-cent stamps alone had been issued, they would not be worth $5.50 and $7 today. In a sense they have benefited from the relative scarcity of the high value in the set. Many collectors, in their zeal to acquire the scarcer 5-cent item, have purchased the entire set at auction, because it was being sold that way. Thus, the demand for the 5-cent has caused increased demand for the two lower values.

ANALYZING THE FAMOUS AMERICANS

A more recent example of key stamps can be found in the 1940 set of 35 portraits of Famous Americans (Scott Nos. 859-893).

I am not wholly convinced of the investment value of these stamps, because they were not issued in the classic period and would not qualify as truly scarce, because they were produced in quantities ranging from 11 million to 58 million apiece.

But it is the very *disparity* of amounts issued that creates the key-stamp concept. You see, these 35 stamps were issued in seven sets, each set consisting of five stamps, one to honor authors, another for educators, and so on. Each five-stamp grouping contains a 1-cent, 2-cent, 3-cent, 5-cent and 10-cent stamp.

Let's take the 1-cent of the authors grouping, which depicts Washington Irving. This had a catalogue value of only 6 cents in 1965, and remained at 6 cents in 1975. However, the high value of the group, the 10-cent stamp depicting Samuel Clemens, went from $1 in 1965 to $2.50 in 1975.

Why? Because the 1-cent was issued in 56 million copies, while the 10-cent was available in only 13 million copies, roughly one-fourth the amount.

The entire 35-stamp set of Famous Americans had a catalogue value of only $22.53 in 1975. Thus, it is well within the reach of every collector. Strong demand will continue. It should rise in value. And the key stamps (the 10-cent stamp of each group) will probably rise fastest of all. The only inhibiting factor is that none of these stamps is very scarce. Perhaps a scarcer variety of these, such as plate number blocks of the 10-cent values, or even full mint sheets, would show more dramatic increases. For example, the plate block of the 10-cent Samuel Clemens (Scott No. 863) had a catalogue value of $20 in 1969; by 1975 it was up to $42.50.

If you will check on the original quantities issued of U.S. stamps, you will see other examples. (The *Scott's U.S. Specialized Catalogue* lists quantities issued for all commemorative and airmail stamps. For quantities issued of definitive stamps, contact the Bureau of Printing and Engraving of the U.S. Treasury Department in Washington, D.C.) Here are just a few early sets, comparing quantities issued of a common stamp in the set and the key stamp in the set, with current market values.

SIX LESSONS IN KEY STAMPS

- Columbian Issue of 1893: 2-cent brown-violet, 1,464,588,750 issued, $6.25; $4 crimson-lake, 27,350 issued, $850.
- Trans-Mississippi Issue of 1898: 1-cent dark yellow-green, 70,993,400 issued, $8.25; $2 orange-brown, 56,200 issued, $725.

- Pan-American Exposition of 1901: 2-cent carmine and black, 209,759,700 issued, $5.25; 8-cent brown-violet, 4,921,700 issued, $42.50.
- Louisiana Purchase Issue of 1904: 2-cent carmine, 192,732,400 issued, $9; 10-cent red-brown, 4,011,200 issued, $87.50.
- Panama-Pacific Issue of 1915: 1-cent green, 334,796,926 issued, $5; 10-cent orange-yellow, 16,968,365 issued, $50.
- Huguenot-Walloon Issue of 1924: 1-cent dark-green, 51,378,023 issued, $2.50; 5-cent dark-blue, 5,348,800 issued, $17.50.

I could go on and on with examples of key stamps, but there's no need to belabor the obvious: When you have a popular set, particularly with low-cost items at the start of the set, this creates a demand for completion. It's like a force of nature. By examining the post office figures of quantities issued for each stamp in the set, you can predict with a fair degree of accuracy which items command high prices and are rising quickly in value. The *Scott Catalogue* prices reflect this demand. Invariably, it is the last stamp in the set, or the last few in a long set, the high values, that are the key stamps.

A 531-PERCENT PRICE APPRECIATION

This is why, for example, the 2-cent stamp of the 1901 Pan-American set has multiplied in value by 262 times over its original post office cost, while the rarer 8-cent brown-violet stamp has multiplied in value by 531 times. The multiplier effect tapers off in the case of high-value stamps such as those that sold at the post office for $2 or $4, because they now are worth hundreds of dollars, and the number of potential buyers thins out, but you can observe the effect quite clearly with a 2-cent stamp and an 8-cent stamp that were printed in very different quantities.

If you have a collection of U.S. stamps, you will naturally want complete sets in order to fill in those blank album spaces. If you have extra money to invest, it should go toward acquiring multiple copies of the key stamps, which are scarcer, and more likely to climb in value.

HOW TO READ THE "X-RATED" TABLES

On the following pages, I list the choice U.S. stamps that have appreciated by 12 percent, 15 percent, 20 percent or more, year after year, in bull and bear markets, in times of boom and in times of recession. I have "x-rated" these stamps with my private system, assigning them values of "1x" to "6x." My x-ratings have nothing to do with pornography. They deal with the healthy multiplication of values.

12-percent growth:

1x stamps have risen in market value by at least 75 percent in the past five years, *or* by 207 percent in the past ten years. This means that they have gone up at least 12 percent per year during *one* of the two periods mentioned.

2x stamps are a little steadier. They have risen in market value by at least 75 percent in the past five years, *and* by 207 percent or more in the past ten years, meaning they have sustained 12-percent annual growth during both periods.

15-percent growth:

3x stamps have gone up 100 percent in five years, *or* 304 percent or more in ten years, signifying 15-percent annual growth in one of the two periods mentioned.

4x stamps have risen 100 percent in five years *and* 304 percent in ten years, a 15-percent annual growth rate in both periods.

20-percent growth:

5x denotes stamps that have risen by 148 percent in the past five years, *or* by 519 percent in ten years, which works out to 20-percent annual growth during one of these two periods.

6x is the top category, for stamps that have risen 148 percent in five years, *and* by 519 percent in ten years, meaning that they have sustained annual growth of 20 percent during both periods.

The stamps are listed in approximate chronological order, with airmails in the final section. After each stamp's x-rating, I list its year of issue, its denomination and a brief description: color, perforation measure, etc. I also include the stamp's *Scott Catalogue* number for easy reference. Next, I offer an estimate of the stamp's present retail cost based on an unused copy in Fine to Very Fine condition. These values can fluctuate sharply, depending upon condition, supply and demand. I merely include them to give you a "ballpark" figure of their worth, and to indicate that some of the best investment choices can be acquired for only a few dollars, while others cost several thousand.

SOME WORDS OF CAUTION

This list does not pretend to be all-inclusive. It is limited to unused U.S. stamps. Gains could also be listed for used stamps, but they tend to be less dramatic. There is also quite a boom in the sale of U.S. plate blocks, but, as I have said, this type of speculation requires great expertise. For this reason, I have limited my prime choices to single stamps, and in a few cases to stamps that are commonly found in joined pairs.

If you want solid investment, as opposed to speculation, my rule of thumb is: Stick to stamps issued before 1925. These are all more than half-a-century old. They are available in finite, relatively modest quantities. They have long-established track records. They have gone up in good times and bad.

If you wish to add a dash of speculation, try acquiring some of my choices up through the year 1939. They, too, have a fairly well established track record.

I view any stamps issued after 1939 as too speculative, unless you can buy them at very attractive discounts. I have listed a number of these, because money is being made on them, but their market positions are not solidly established. Some may be overpriced.

Let me call your attention, for example, to the 1962 Project Mercury stamp. It went up 275 percent in 10 years. But between 1974 and 1975 its value dropped by 14.5 percent, a very rare phenomenon in the stamp world. This stamp may make money in the long run, but one must be careful. I don't recall ever having seen such a dramatic drop in value for older stamps. My x-rated tables of high-yield stamps follow.

	Gain in Value by Percentage				
U.S. Stamps at 1975 Retail Value	10 years	5 years	1972-1973	1973-1974	1974-1975
(3x) 1847 5c red-brown, imperf (#1) $300	270.4	100.0	12.5	0	11.1
(3x) 1847 10c black, imperf (#2) $1300	500.0	130.8	35.1	9.1	9.1
(4x) 1851 3c orange-brown, imperf (#10) $140	358.3	107.7	8.1	12.5	22.2
(1x) 1857 3c dull-red, perf 15. (#26) $7	277.3	66.7	0	12.5	11.1
1875 government reprints, white paper without gum, perf 12:					
(4x) 3c scarlet (#41) $900 ...	433.3	118.2	12.5	11.1	20.0
(3x) 10c blue-green (#43) $600	433.3	77.7	9.1	16.7	14.3

U.S. Stamps at 1975 Retail Value	10 years	5 years	1972-1973	1973-1974	1974-1975
(3x) 30c yellow-orange (#46) $900	321.0	60.0	5.3	10.0	9.1
(3x) 90c deep-blue (#47) $1400	385.7	70.0	0	11.5	17.2
1869 pictorial issue, perf 12:					
(3x) 6c ultramarine (#115) $110	311.7	94.4	0	12.0	35.0
(2x) 10c yellow (#116) $125 .	289.4	89.7	0	22.0	12.1
(2x) 12c green (#117) $110 ..	266.6	83.3	0	20.0	10.0
(2x) 15c brown & blue (#119) $140	300.0	81.8	3.4	26.7	5.3
(3x) 24c green & violet (#120) $400	313.0	90.0	7.1	6.7	18.7
(1x) 30c blue & carmine (#121) $400	270.3	66.7	6.2	0	17.6
(4x) 90c carmine & black (#122) $1,000	330.8	100.0	11.1	25.0	12.0
(1x) 1870 30c black white wove paper, perf 12, (#143) $900	285.9	62.3	5.9	11.1	10.0
1870 white wove paper without grill, perf 12:					
(2x) 12c dull-violet (#151) $100	275.0	76.5	0	8.3	15.4
(2x) 30c black (#154) $150 ..	233.0	87.5	7.1	11.1	20.0
(3x) 1879 6c pink perf 12 (#186) $80	300.0	100.0	15.8	13.6	20.0
(2x) 1890 2c carmine (#220) $2.50	282.3	75.7	6.4	10.0	18.2
(2x) 1890 90c orange (#229) $75	233.5	90.5	8.0	18.5	25.0
(3x) 1893 Columbian Exposition, 1c to $5, 16 values (#230-245) $3,000	367.1	91.5	5.5	12.1	19.4
Individual items in Columbian set:					
(2x) 1c deep-blue (#230) $6...	250.0	75.0	0	22.2	27.3

U.S. Stamps at 1975 Retail Value	10 years	5 years	1972-1973	1973-1974	1974-1975
(1x) 2c violet (#231) $5	237.8	66.7	0	17.6	25.0
(1x) 3c green (#232) $12	250.0	64.7	0	31.6	12.0
(2x) 4c ultramarine (#233) $13	247.8	82.6	0	20.0	33.3
(2x) 5c chocolate (#234) $17 .	261.5	88.0	3.7	25.0	34.3
(2x) 6c purple (#235) $17 ...	235.0	74.0	0	16.6	34.3
(3x) 10c black-brown (#237) $25	294.7	108.3	6.7	18.7	31.6
(2x) 15c dark-green (#238) $45	259.4	76.9	0	18.7	21.0
(2x) 30c orange-brown (#239) $60	300.0	77.7	0	18.2	23.1
(2x) 50c slate-blue (#240) $100	242.9	71.4	5.9	11.0	20.0
(3x) $1 salmon (#241) $275 .	311.7	75.0	0	20.0	16.7
(3x) $2 brown-red (#242) $320	305.3	67.4	3.4	11.7	14.9
(3x) $3 yellow-green (#243) $400	346.4	92.3	5.9	11.1	25.0
(4x) $4 crimson-lake (#244) $650	466.0	112.5	8.3	11.5	17.2
(4x) $5 black (#245) $750 ...	429.4	100.0	7.7	10.7	16.1
1894 Unwatermarked, perf 12:					
(3x) 2c carmine-lake, type I (#249) $15	335.2	85.0	0	11.1	23.3
(4x) 2c carmine, type II (#251) $35	350.0	125.0	13.2	25.0	20.0
(3x) 50c orange (#260) $50 ..	257.1	92.3	0	17.6	25.0
(2x) 1895, similar to 1894 issue but with double-lined USPS watermark. 2c carmine, type I (#265) $5	285.7	80.0	0	15.8	22.7
(2x) 1898 Trans-Mississippi Exposition, perf 12, 1c to $2, 9 values (#285-293) $1,650	298.1	93.4	2.9	17.1	24.1

U.S. Stamps at 1975 Retail Value	10 years	5 years	1972-1973	1973-1974	1974-1975
Selected individual items from Trans-Mississippi set:					
(2x) 4c orange (#287) $30 ...	226.0	87.5	4.2	14.0	31.6
(2x) 8c violet-brown (#289) $38	251.8	90.0	0	33.0	18.7
(2x) 10c gray-violet (#290) $45	242.8	71.4	0	31.2	14.3
(2x) 50c sage-green (#291) $160	275.0	80.0	3.4	23.3	21.6
(2x) $1 black (#292) $450 ...	284.6	88.7	0	21.4	17.6
(4x) $2 orange-brown (#293) $600	339.4	107.1	5.3	30.0	11.5
(2x) 1901 Pan-American Exposition, 1c to 10c, 6 values (#294-299) $120	236.0	86.7	0	38.5	18.3
Selected individual items from Pan-American set:					
(3x) 8c brown-violet & black (#298) $30	286.3	112.5	0	27.6	41.7
(2x) 10c yellow-brown & black (#299) $42	243.7	83.3	0	24.3	26.4
1903 perf 12, watermarked USPS:					
(1x) 15c olive-green (#309) $35	196.0	86.0	0	20.0	30.0
(3x) 50c orange (#310) $85 ..	238.4	100.0	3.7	17.8	33.3
(2x) $1 black (#311) $150 ...	216.7	90.0	0	20.0	26.6
(2x) 1909 coil, perf 12 vertical, 5c blue (#355) $35	275.0	97.4	6.3	40.0	7.1
(3x) 1909 Hudson-Fulton Celebration 2c carmine, imperf (#373) $18	206.6	109.1	0	34.6	31.4
(5x) 1911 2c carmine, imperf (#384) $1.75	511.0	189.5	0	23.3	48.6
(3x) 1910 coil, 1c green, perf 8½ horizontal (#390) 95 cents	300.0	150.0	0	50.0	33.3

U.S. Stamps at 1975 Retail Value	10 years	5 years	1972-1973	1973-1974	1974-1975
(5x) 1913 coil, 5c blue, perf 8½ vertical (#396) $18	457.9	211.8	17.4	48.1	32.5
(4x) 1912 2c carmine, type I, coil, perf 8½ horizontal (#411) $2	309.1	104.5	0	16.6	28.6
(4x) 1915 2c red, type I rotary-press coil, perf 10 horizontal (#449) $450	450.0	100.0	0	12.5	22.2
(5x) 1914 1c green, rotary-press coil, perf 10 vertical (#452) $2.50	450.0	243.7	0	60.0	37.5
(6x) 1914 coil, 2c carmine, type II (#454) $55	3,839.0	828.6	14.3	50.0	8.3
(6x) 1916 2c carmine, type II rotary coil, perf 10 horizontal (#487) $6.....	2,733.0	750.0	25.0	46.7	54.5
(3x) 1919 2c carmine, type III rotary coil, perf 10 horizontal (#488) 60 cents	400.0	87.5	0	30.0	15.4
(6x) 1917 3c violet, type I rotary coil, perf 10 vertical (#493) $11	2,900.0	650.0	0	100.0	36.4
(6x) 1918 3c violet, type II rotary coil, perf 10 vertical (#494) $5	1,344.0	306.2	6.4	110.0	23.8
(5x) 1917 3c deep-rose, type Ia, flat plate, perf 11 (#500) $80	962.5	88.8	7.1	13.3	0
(3x) 1920 2c carmine, type IV, offset, perf 11 (#526) $5	283.3	130.0	7.6	14.3	43.7
(2x) 1922-1925, perf 11, 23 values from ½c to $5 (#551-573) $200	214.7	88.9	0	40.4	13.3
Selected individual items from 1922-1925 set:					
(2x) 5c dark-blue (#557) $5...	250.0	75.0	4.4	28.6	16.6
(3x) 30c olive-brown (#569) $7	300.0	100.0	0	35.0	18.5

U.S. Stamps at 1975 Retail Value	10 years	5 years	1972-1973	1973-1974	1974-1975
(3x) $5 carmine & blue (#573) $80	294.8	138.1	0	80.0	11.1
(6x) 1929 2c carmine, type II, rotary coil, perf 10 vertical (#599A) $75	575.0	170.0	12.5	38.9	8.0
(6x) 1924 3c violet, rotary coil, perf 10 vertical (#600) $2.95	1,650.0	400.0	12.5	288.9	0
(2x) 1925 Lexington-Concord set, 5c dark-blue, perf 11 (#619) $16	275.0	93.5	0	25.7	36.4
(5x) 1928 2c carmine, type II, rotary, perf 11x10½ (#634A) $150	554.0	93.3	4.5	17.4	7.4
(4x) 1929 2c carmine-rose, rotary coil, perf 10 vertical (#656) $9	390.0	107.7	12.5	38.9	8.0
(5x) 1933 APS Souvenir Sheets, 1c deep-yellow-green & 3c deep-violet, imperf (#730-731) $40	334.0	161.5	10.2	61.1	14.9
(3x) 1938-1954, 32 values from ½c to $5, perf 11x10½ (#803-834) $70	276.9	144.7	4.1	47.1	31.8
Selected items from above set:					
(5x) 50c light-red-violet (#831) $4	300.0	185.7	0	55.5	42.8
(1x) $1 purple & black (#832) $3.50	144.4	83.3	0	19.4	37.5
(4x) $5 carmine & black (#834) $50	420.8	247.2	8.7	80.0	38.9
(6x) 1939 Presidential set, rotary coil, 13 values from 1c to 10c (#839-851) $20	1,200.0	497.7	11.1	79.9	4.0
Selected items from Presidential set:					
(3x) 1c green, perf 10 vertical (#839) 14 cents	300.0	100.0	0	33.0	0

U.S. Stamps at 1975 Retail Value	10 years	5 years	1972-1973	1973-1974	1974-1975
(6x) 4c red-violet, perf 10 vertical (#843) $4.75	2,955.	1,122.	33.3	150.	10
(6x) 5c bright-blue, perf 10 vertical (#845) $2.50	1,844.	900.	56.2	140.	16.7
(6x) 10c brown-red, perf 10 vertical (#847) $10; $31 a pair	2,100.	780.	0	46.7	0
(6x) 1c green, perf 10 horizontal (#848) 30 cents; 75 cents a pair	566.	233.3	25.	60.	0
(6x) 2c green, perf 10 horizontal (#850) $1; $1.75 a pair	816.7	266.7	12.5	144.4	0
(6x) 3c deep-violet, perf 10 horizontal (#851) $1; $3.25 a pair	733.	257.1	9.1	108.3	0
(3x) 1948 Fort Bliss Centennial 3c henna-brown (#976) 15 cents	150.	150.	33.3	25.	0
(5x) 1960 Echo I 4c deep-violet (#1173) 28 cents	462.5	462.5	25.0	40.	28.6
(5x) 1962 Project Mercury 4c dark-blue & yellow (#1193) 17 cents	275.	275.	25.	40.	-14.3
(5x) 1967 Prominent Americans 1¼c green (#1279) 5 cents .	—	566.6	0	0	100.
(5x) 1967 Space Twins, Joined pair of multicolor stamps, 5c each (#1331a) $3	—	1,650.	100.	16.7	0
(3x) 1968 Historic Flags, set of 10 6c values (#1345-1354) $2; strip of 10 joined, $3 ...	—	108.3	0	33.	25.
(5x) 1969 Beautification, set of 4 6c values (#1365-1368) $3	—	525.0	20.	233.3	25.
(5x) 1969 Apollo 8 6c black, blue & ochre (#1371) 22 cents	—	150.	33.	50.	0
(2x) 1969 Botanical Congress, set of 4 6c stamps (#1376-1379) $1	—	—	20.0	10.	25.

•

U.S. Stamps at 1975 Retail Value	10 years	5 years	1972- 1973	1973- 1974	1974- 1975
U.S. Airmail Issues at 1975 Retail Value					
(3x) 1918 6c orange (#C1) $30 .	311.7	94.4	2.2	41.3	7.7
(2x) 1918 16c green (#C2) $60 .	263.6	90.5	1.3	25.	23.7
(3x) 1918 24c carmine-rose (#C3) $50	334.6	79.2	7.7	50.	9.5
(4x) 1923 16c dark-blue (#C5) $50	334.6	119.2	6.6	56.2	15.0
(4x) 1923 24c carmine (# C6) $60	306.	113.1	94.6	34.7	34.0
(3x) 1926–1927 10c dark-blue, 15c olive-brown & 20c yellow-green (# C7-C9) $7.50	285.4	116.4	10.	25.4	14.5
(3x) 1927 Lindbergh plane 10c dark-blue (#C10) $3 ..	170.8	103.1	6.9	22.2	18.2
(3x) 1928 5c carmine & black (#C11) $1.95	246.1	125.	8.	37.	21.6
(3x) 1930 5c violet (#C12) $6 ..	300.	100.	20.	16.7	0
(3x) 1932 8c olive-bistre (#C17) 80 cents	122.	100.	7.7	14.3	25.
(3x) 1935–1937 25c blue, 20c green & 50c carmine, China Clipper set (#C20-C22) $10	300.	108.7	10.3	33.1	12.7
(3x) 1939 30c dull-blue (#C24) $6	180.	100.	5.	40.	0
(1x) 1941 20c bright-green (#C29) 90 cents	107.7	92.8	5.6	44.4	0
(1x) 1941 50c orange (#C31) $4	197.3	122.2	7.7	21.4	29.4
(5x) 1964 8c blue, red & bistre Goddard rocket (#C69) 60 cents	—	350.	50.	100.	0
(5x) 1968 10c blue, black & red Curtiss Jenny (#C74) 25 cents	—	200.	14.3	37.5	9.1

A CAUTIONARY WORD ABOUT THE RATINGS

The fact that a stamp is rated 5x or 6x in these tables doesn't necessarily mean that I view it as a better investment than a 3x or 4x stamp. To reemphasize: The ratings reflect *past* performance only; I cannot predict the future.

You'll note that many of the 5x and 6x stamps are of relatively recent vintage, so they must be viewed as somewhat speculative. Were I to invest important amounts of money, I would feel far more confident with 3x or 4x items in Fine or better condition that are of pre-1900, or at least pre-1920, vintage. As you can see from the tables, such older items have long histories of stable growth and are less subject to up-and-down swings.

PLATE BLOCKS: BOOM OR BUST?

While we're on the subject of caution, I'd like to warn you about the current upsurge in values for plate number blocks of U.S. stamps. The ads for these run fast and furious in the philatelic press, but I doubt that many knowledgeable collector/investors are biting.

There has always been a strong market for truly scarce plate blocks, but these are usually blocks of the same stamps that are good investments when purchased as singles. Today many ordinarily common stamps, when sold in plate block form, are selling for inflated prices. Be careful!

Let's take the 3-cent Will Rogers stamp of 1948 (Scott No. 975). Many retail ads now offer plate blocks of these at $1 apiece. But at the same time the Harris Company offers to buy them back for only 28 cents. This is far too wide a gap between "buy" and "sell." The ads neglect to mention that 67 million of these stamps were issued, meaning that plate blocks of this item are not scarce at all.

Another supposedly red-hot item in the current plate block craze is the 1968 U.S. Historic Flags issue (Scott Nos. 1345-1354). Plate blocks of these are sold in units of 20 stamps, with a face value of $1.20. Current retail ads offer this plate block for about $14.50. The Harris Company will buy them back from you for $8. As you can see, it will take quite some time for this stamp to appreciate to the point where you will earn a profit. When you consider the fact that more than 4.6 million of these plate blocks were put into circulation by the U.S. Post Office, you will understand why I believe their current prices are inflated. You can still purchase these plate blocks "per 100" from some retailers. If they are so plentiful, imagine what will happen when you try to sell them back.

Obviously, their current retail price is caused by dealer promotion, and not by collector demand. If there is ever a "crash" in the philatelic market, the first victims will be collectors of modern plate blocks.

SOME PRICE TRENDS IN U.S. PLATE BLOCKS

Description/ Date/ Scott No.	Post Office Value	1975 Catalogue Value ("Sell")	1975 Dealer Price ("Buy")
5c Space Twins, 1967 (#1331-1332) block of 4	$ .20	$17.50	$6.00
6c Historic Flags, 1968 (#1345-1354) block of 20	1.20	17.50	8.00
6c Wildlife Conservation, 1968 (#1362) block of 4	.24	3.25	1.10
6c Beautification, 1969 (#1365-1368) block of 4	.24	12.50	4.00
6c Botanical Congress, 1969 (#1376-1379) block of 4	.24	13.50	4.90

Description/Date/Scott No.	Post Office Value	1975 Catalogue Value ("Sell")	1975 Dealer Price ("Buy")
8c Postal Service, 1971 (#1396) block of 12 ...	.96	5.25	3.10
6c Anti-Pollution, 1970 (#1410-1413) block of 10	.60	8.00	3.00
6c Christmas Toys, 1970 (#1415-1418) block of 8	.48	10.00	3.00

The above table, showing current catalogue values for some recent plate blocks, and current "buy" prices, illustrates the unpleasantly wide disparity between "buy" and "sell."

Had you purchased some of these items at the post office, you would, of course, stand to make a handsome profit. But who, at the time, could predict that these stamps would rise in value, while many others of the same period did not? Remember: There is no simple formula for post-1940 stamps.

Also remember that in order to acquire a plate block at the post office you must usually buy the entire sheet of 50 stamps. To acquire a plate block of four 10-cent stamps, you would have to lay out $5 for the entire sheet. What do you do with the rest of the stamps?

HOW TO GET PLATE BLOCKS PAINLESSLY

If you have a business that requires lots of postage, buy sheets of commemoratives, detach the plate blocks and store them away in glassine envelopes. Use the rest for postage.

If you know someone whose business requires a large mail volume, offer to supply his stamp needs, detach the plate blocks for yourself, and sell the others to him at face value. In this way, you can acquire some plate blocks painlessly, with little investment.

Some earlier plate block material is supported by strong "buy" prices. You should be aware of these "buy/sell" ratios before you contemplate investing. If you insist upon pursuing the field of plate blocks, you should certainly acquire a *Durland Standard Plate Number Catalogue,* for reference purposes. You should also have a *Crane List,* which quotes retail prices for all U.S. plate blocks from 1935 to the present. Also useful is Clark-Smith's *Current Plate Block Prices,* published ten times a year, at $7.50 (write to C.S.E., Box 5526, Columbus, Ohio 43221), with sample copies available for $2.

You might also spend $1 for a sample copy of the *Plate Block Investment Advisory Newsletter* (Dr. Robert Rabinowitz, 37 Stanwick Place, Stamford, Conn. 06905). I have not used this newsletter's advice, but it will at least expose you to some informed thinking on this subject. Another source of data is *The Marketeer,* a weekly pocket-sized publication which costs $1.50 per issue, or $52 per year (from International Stamp Collectors Association, 2172 E. 54th St., Indianapolis, Indiana 46220). This gives weekly "buy/sell" prices for U.S. plate blocks and mint sheets, compiled by computer.

As I mentioned before, the better plate-block investments are probably in those same classic and middle period stamps that climb rapidly in value even as single stamps. You can chart their changes in value by referring to previous editions of *Scott's U.S. Specialized Catalogues.*

Plate blocks issued prior to 1920 are very scarce and command high prices. For example, the catalogue value of a single 10-cent Columbian stamp of 1893 (Scott No. 237) has gone up from $16 to $37.50 between 1969 and 1975. During the same period, a plate block of that stamp has risen from $235 to $700.

For earlier issues, be sure to check how many stamps

make up a block. In previous years, certain stamps were commonly collected in blocks of six, eight or twelve stamps. *Scott's U.S. Specialized Catalogue* supplies this information.

Now, let's explore the investment possibilities for stamps from other parts of the world.

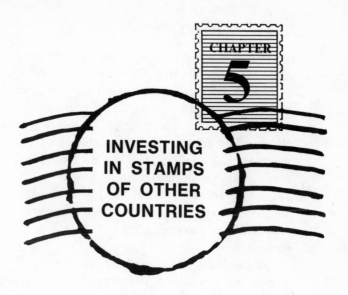

CHAPTER

5

**INVESTING
IN STAMPS
OF OTHER
COUNTRIES**

As I have mentioned, U.S. stamps are probably the safest for the new collector/investor because the market for stamps is usually strongest in the country of origin. The fluctuation of foreign exchange rates is another factor to be considered. However, once you have become reasonably familiar with the world of philately, you may want to explore opportunities abroad.

For the sake of convenience, you may want to begin with those countries listed in Volume I of the *Scott Catalogue*, which, in addition to stamps of the United States, includes those of the United Nations and the far-flung British Commonwealth.

HOW TO BUY UNITED NATIONS STAMPS

Investment choices here are limited, because the UN only began issuing stamps as recently as 1951; there can only be a few truly scarce "classics."

UN stamps are used on official and private mail sent from UN headquarters in New York or from the UN's European office in Geneva. The UN issues its own stamp catalogue (50,000 copies sold last year) and has thousands of mail-order clients who subscribe to a new-issue stamp service. Collectors in Switzerland and Western Europe create a steady demand for UN-Geneva issues, which are issued in Swiss currency denominations.

Perhaps the single highest-priced item of UN philately is an unique imperforate sheet of the 25-cent black airmail issue of 1951. This sheet was recently offered in a private treaty sale in New York for a minimum bid of $275,000, or about $5,500 per stamp.

Because the UN is so young and has issued relatively few stamps, one can become fairly expert in their growth rate with relatively little study.

The most expensive regular item in the UN portfolio is the 1955 UN Charter souvenir sheet (Scott No. 38), which catalogued at a mere $40 in 1965 and is now up to about $200, having appreciated more than $60 in just a few months of 1975.

In general, the earliest issues are strongest, particularly the first regular and airmail sets, both of which were issued in 1951. Here is a list of a few promising UN stamps:

	1965 catalogue value	1975 catalogue value	1975 approximate dealer prices	
Date/Description/Scott No.			buy	sell
1951 first set of eleven stamps (Scott Nos. 1-11)	$4.65	$22.55	$9.00	$12.50
3c bright-blue and 5c rose-red Human Rights Day of 1953 (Scott Nos. 21-22)	1.10	4.75	2.00	3.00

Date/Description/Scott No.	1965 catalogue value	1975 catalogue value	1975 approximate dealer prices buy	sell
3c blue and 8c rose-carmine Symbol of Flight, 1955 (Scott Nos. 31-32)	1.70	7.25	2.50	4.00
3c lilac-rose and 8c light-blue UNESCO emblem, 1955 (Scott Nos. 33-34)	1.30	4.25	1.00	1.50
First four airmails, 1951 (Scott Nos. C1-C4) ..	1.35	5.80	2.00	2.75

These prices, while they will be obsolete by the time you read this, do give you an idea of stamp trends, showing how some have multiplied in value. They also offer an example of the difference between "catalogue value" (columns 1 and 2) and "retail price" (column 4), which is also different from the dealer's "buy price" (column 3). We'll discuss pricing in far greater detail later on, but I can't emphasize too often that catalogue value should not be confused with actual "buy" and "sell" prices.

THE HALF CATALOGUE RULE

You'll notice that the retail "sell" price for these UN stamps is roughly half of the current catalogue value. Most collectors expect to buy their unused stamps for what is known as "half Scott" or "half catalogue." This is a cozy rule, but it can be dangerous. While it holds true for these UN items, other rare stamps—nineteenth-century U.S., for instance—often sell for three-quarters of the catalogue value or more. Stamps of many other nations, for example, much of Central and South America, can frequently be acquired for one-fourth, even one-tenth, of the catalogue value. Confusing? Yes. But after a bit of study, you'll discern a pattern.

Other items to watch in the UN are its postal stationery. For example, the UN Geneva airletter (UC1) was issued in 1969 in a relatively small quantity: 350,000. This item had only limited usage and went off sale in the summer of 1971. In a single year, its value jumped from 35 cents to $5.

Wars, too, have created UN rarities. Special airletters were created for troops in the UN Emergency Force I in the Middle East conflict and for the UN Disengagement Observer Force (UNDOF). These exist in limited quantities and are snapped up by UN specialists.

If the UN attracts you, you might consider the possibility of acquiring an entire country collection. In early 1974, one major retailer was offering the UN's first 233 regular stamps and 18 airmails for $285 in unused condition. Within this amount, the 1955 Souvenir Sheet (Scott No. 38), which catalogued for $200, was valued at $145. Just a year later, the same retailer was offering the complete UN collection for $315. In mid-1975 you could still get this "country collection" for less than $315, but the market quotations show that in one year the value of the collection rose by more than 10 percent.

If you were to buy the entire UN collection, and then keep it current by purchasing new issues at face value from UN headquarters in New York, chances are that your investment would grow substantially over the years. You could also derive some aesthetic pleasure from this enterprise by mounting the collection in an album. Then, you could purchase multiple copies of the more valuable items (such as the 1955 Souvenir Sheet) and store them for safekeeping.

CANADA: A GOOD INVESTMENT OPPORTUNITY

Stamps of neighboring Canada offer a very fertile field for the collector/investor. During 1974, early Canadian stamps up to the 1920s were commanding auction prices 20 percent higher than the previous year. The $5 olive-green of 1897 (Scott No. 65) was up by *34 percent* in a year's time! Even the 11-stamp set of June 1935 (Scott Nos. 217-227), despite its relative newness, went up by 27 percent over the previous year.

The Scott Company plans to publish a specialized catalogue of Canadian stamps. Scott's current listing for Canada includes values only for single unused and used stamps. The new catalogue would also show prices for pairs, plate blocks, and other specialties. This move by Scott will almost certainly enhance the value of Canadian stamps among U.S. collectors, and it merits your attention.

Here are a few examples of early Canadian stamps, unused, that have risen dramatically in price during the past decade:

	Catalogue Value	
Description/Date/Scott No.	*1965*	*1975*
3p red, 1858 (#12)	$210.00	$600.00
6p brown-violet, 1859 (#13)	900.00	3,000.00
5c vermilion, 1859 (#15)	25.00	70.00
1c yellow-orange, 1868 (#23)	75.00	250.00
5c olive-green, 1875 (#26)	55.00	150.00
½c black, 1882 (#34)	.40	2.00
10c dull rose-lilac, 1877 (#40)	27.50	75.00
50c deep-blue, 1892 (#47)	16.00	75.00

Also worth looking into is the entire Jubilee Issue of 1897 (Scott Nos. 50-65), which is the Canadian equivalent in prestige of the U.S. Columbian Issue of 1893. Some of the fastest-rising items in this set are the ½-cent black, from $5 to $20; the 6-cent yellow-brown, from $10 to $40; the $1 lake, from $50 to $175; the $3 yellow-bistre, from $100 to $400; and the $5 olive-green, from $100 to $425.

I particularly like the high values, from $1 up, which were issued in smaller quantities and are key stamps.

GREAT BRITAIN: WELL WORTH INVESTIGATING

This, as you know, is the home of the world's first postage stamp, the famed Penny Black of 1840, showing a profile of Queen Victoria. The combination of Great Britain's long history of issuing stamps, and the demand generated by the British public, makes that nation's issues quite attractive to the collector/investor. If you make the ten-year comparison test of *Scott Catalogue* values, you will find dozens of items that are worth investigating.

Late in 1974, the Gibbons Company issued the seventy-seventh edition of its *British Commonwealth Stamp Catalogue,* which showed increases in a year's time of 25 percent for stamps issued during the reigns of Queen Victoria and King Edward VII, and 20 percent for those issued during the reign of George V.

Gibbons also publishes a booklet, *Collect British Stamps,* in a quantity of about one million copies, which gives you an idea of the tremendous interest in philately in England. The booklet notes price increases of "hundreds of pounds" for some items. One of the many items singled out for its vigorous growth is the 1929 one-pound black Postal Union stamp, which stayed at face value until World War II and then crept up to two pounds sterling, stayed there for ten more years, and is now listed at 125 pounds. The *Scott Catalogues* offer a barometer of the British stamp market. Here is a random sampling:

Description/ Date/ Scott No.	1965	1975
1-pence black Queen Victoria, 1840 (# 1)	$ 95.00	$350.00
1-pence red-brown Queen Victoria, 1855 (# 16) ...	5.00	15.00
4-pence bluish-rose Queen Victoria, 1855 (# 22) ..	185.00	500.00
1½-pence lilac-rose Queen Victoria, 1860 (# 31) ...	110.00	375.00
1-pound brown-violet Queen Victoria, 1884 (# 110)	385.00	1,250.00
1-shilling carmine-rose & green Queen Victoria, 1900 (# 126)	2.00	18.00
1-pound green King Edward VII, 1902 (# 142)	40.00	300.00
Three-stamp set of Britannia Rules the Waves, 1919 (# 179-181)	22.00	93.50
Three-stamp set of Britannia Rules the Waves, 1934 (# 222-224)	28.50	137.50
1-pound deep-chalky-blue King George VI and Queen Elizabeth, 1948 (# 268)	6.00	20.00

And this is just a tiny sampling of British stamps that have experienced healthy price increases. A reminder: If you plan to invest in British stamps, you should definitely acquire a *Gibbons Catalogue* published in England to supplement the price information provided by the U.S.-published *Scott Catalogue*.

You'll notice that most of the rewarding items date back to the nineteenth century, or around the turn of the century. The most recent stamp I've listed was issued in 1948. Few stamps of such recent vintage have done as well. That same year (1948), Great Britain issued a set of four stamps to publicize the Olympic Games held at Wembley. In 1965 the set catalogued for 97 cents. Ten years later it was $1.50, hardly enough to compensate for inflation. British Commonwealth investment opportunities will be considered individually.

The members of the British Commonwealth of Nations constitute a vast domain, past and present, stretching all over the globe, from the tiny islands of the West Indies, to the emerging nations of Africa, to the vast stretches of Australia. The great number of British collectors assures a steady market for many of these items, but the stamp-issuing policies of each nation and colony (particularly in recent years) vary widely. This is why you must be very selective in choosing British Commonwealth stamps for investment. But there are many opportunities.

AUSTRALIA

Australia, for example, is so large and well developed that it has created its own local stamp market and its own catalogues. Prices are climbing constantly. Even the ugly half-pence Kangaroo of 1913, Australia's first stamp, has risen in value from 20 cents to $1.35 in a decade. Here is a sampler of Australian items that merit your attention:

	Catalogue Value	
Description/Date/Scott No.	*1965*	*1975*
5-pence orange-brown Kangaroo, 1913 (#7)	$ 3.75	$ 17.50
2-shilling brown Kangaroo, 1913 (#11)	9.00	50.00
10-shilling pink & gray Kangaroo, 1913 (#13)	40.00	240.00
1-pound ultramarine & brown Kangaroo, 1913 (#14)	110.00	750.00
2-pound deep-rose & black Kangaroo, 1913 (#15) .	200.00	1,100.00
1-shilling, 4-pence pale-turquoise-blue King George V, 1928 (#76)	3.75	22.50

Excuse the pun, but you can see that some of those early Kangaroos have been really leaping ahead. I haven't listed recent Australian material, but it also deserves attention. You might, for example, look at the Military Stamps of 1946-1947 (Scott Nos. M1-M7), which were overprinted with the initials of the British Occupation Forces in Japan. In a decade, these went from $13.45 to $37.05.

WEST INDIES: WATCH THE EARLY ISSUES

Most recent stamps of the British West Indies are exotic-looking, but only so-so for investment because they have been issued in large quantities. However, earlier issues often command high prices at auction, and reflect strong increases in value.

- The 1862 6-pence blue-green Queen Victoria of Antigua (Scott No. 1), for example, has gone up from $95 to $300.
- In the Bahamas, the 1-shilling green and black King George V of 1912 (Scott No. 56) has gone from $30 to $90.
- From Bermuda, the 10-shilling red and green King George V of 1924 (Scott No. 96) is up from $14 to $47.50.
- In the Cayman Islands, check on the 1-shilling brown and orange King Edward VII of 1905 (Scott No. 12), up from $8 to $24. And the 10-shilling green and red of the same monarch, issued in 1908 (Scott No. 30), up from $32.50 to $100.
- The island of Dominica also has some promising items. Try, for example, the 1-pound violet and black Seal of Colony and King George V of 1923 (Scott No. 85), up from $30 to $120 in a decade's time.
- The so-called "spice island" of Grenada is one of the worst offenders in issuing too many current stamps. But its nineteenth-century stamps are authentically scarce. One example is the 10-shilling red and green Seal of Colony of 1908 (Scott No. 78), which rose in a decade from $22.50 to $75.

THE DANISH WEST INDIES (U.S. VIRGIN ISLANDS): AN ATTRACTIVE PORTFOLIO

While we're touring the Caribbean, I don't want to ignore the Danish West Indies, which were sold to the United States in 1917 and are now the U.S. Virgin Islands. You'll find these old Danish colonial stamps listed a few pages after U.S. stamps in your *Scott Catalogue.*

Danish West Indies stamps were issued between 1855 and 1917. *Many* of them have jumped in value. In fact, if you could acquire the entire collection, you'd have an attractive investment portfolio at a quite modest price. A few examples:

	Catalogue Value	
Description/ Date/ Scott No.	*1965*	*1975*
4c dull-blue Coat of Arms, 1873 (#4)	$ 20.00	$100.00
7c lilac & orange Numeral of Value, 1873 (#9) ...	2.00	13.00
King Christian IX set of 1905, six stamps (#31-36) .	3.00	22.50
King Frederik VIII set of 1908, eight stamps (#43-50)	6.55	26.45
Postage Due set of 1902, four stamps (#J1–J4) ...	5.10	24.00

CANAL ZONE AND HAWAII

The U.S. section of the *Scott Catalogue* also lists the Canal Zone, which is leased by the United States from the Republic of Panama. Not all of its issues have risen sharply. But take a look at the 2-cent orange-vermilion and black Cordoba overprint of 1915 (Scott No. 47), which in 1965 catalogued for a mere $13.50 and in ten years' time soared to $400. More modest, but also impressive, has been the track record of the 15-cent on 1-cent green airmail stamp of 1929 (Scott No. C2), which went from $4.50 to $35.

Also in the U.S. section of the *Scott Catalogue* you'll find Hawaii, which issued stamps from 1853 through 1899. Look, for example, at the 5-cent blue King Kamehameha III of 1853 (Scott No. 5) which went from $165 to $550 in ten years. Or the five-stamp set depicting Hawaiian royalty, issued between 1864 and 1871 (Scott Nos. 30-34), whose value jumped from $12.85 to $57.50.

MALTA, NEW ZEALAND, KUWAIT, ETC.

In the British Commonwealth, each former colony must be checked with care, including tiny Malta. Its first stamp, the ½-pence buff of 1861, showing the ubiquitous Queen Victoria profile, has risen from $80 to $250 in the past ten years. Some of Malta's more recent issues also merit a look. I refer you to the seventeen-stamp set of 1956–57. And most specifically to the two high values of that set: the 10-shilling dark-carmine (Scott No. 261) went from $2.80 to $15 in a decade; the 1-pound yellow-brown (Scott No. 262) went from $5.60 to $25.

Among the stamps of New Zealand, I suggest you examine the 6-pence gray-green and rose Annexation of 1906 (Scott No. 125), up from $15 to $42.50.

As for South African stamps, try the 1-pound red and deep green King George V of 1916, up from $55 to $225.

Many collectors are fascinated by exotic places, such as the tiny oil sheikdom of Kuwait, a British protectorate until 1961. It doesn't offer numerous investment choices, but look at the 10-rupee carmine and green of 1923, up from $10 to $52.50 in a decade. For more items, try the 1963 Flags set of three (Scott No. 200-203), which has leaped from 46 cents to $6.40.

Another exotic favorite is Gibraltar. I refer you to Gibraltar's 1-pound orange and black King George V of 1927 (Scott No. 92), up from $17.50 to $80. Or the next highest value in that set, the 5-pound dull-violet and black of 1925 (Scott No. 93), up from $175 to $600.

The Republic of Iraq is still listed under the "British Commonwealth" section in the *Scott Catalogue* because it was under British rule from 1920 to 1932. Stamps issued during that period are the most promising investments, because they interest a large sector of British philatelists. Look, for example, at the 25-rupee violet King Faisal I of 1931 (Scott No. 27), up from $65 to $200.

THE COOK AND FALKLAND ISLANDS

Other small, exotic areas whose early stamps command good prices are the Cook Islands of the South Pacific, which are linked to New Zealand, and the Falkland Islands, a British Crown Colony 300 miles east of the Straits of Magellan. Perhaps British and American philatelists enjoy the vicarious thrill of "visiting" these remote spots when they acquire their stamps. Whatever the reason, market demand is strong.

The 10-pence carmine of 1892 of the Cook Islands (Scott No. 4) has gone up from $11 to $42.50 in a decade. The more recent 1927 set of two stamps (Scott Nos. 76-77) has moved nicely from $1.45 to $4.25. There are numerous other examples in between those years, many of which can still be purchased for a few dollars.

In the Falkland Islands, check the 5-shilling dull-red King Edward VII of 1905 (Scott No. 29), up from $15 to $60. Or the 5-shilling yellow and black King Penguin of 1933 (Scott No. 74), up from $40 to $175.

TRY THE IRISH PROVISIONALS

The Republic of Ireland began issuing stamps in 1922, and the earliest ones were "provisionals" that were overprinted on the stamps of Great Britain. Some of these are very scarce. Also in great demand are the first stamps with purely Irish designs. These can sometimes be acquired for less than a dollar, but their values are on the rise. You'll find few more spectacular increases than the 1-shilling light-blue Sword of Light of 1922 (Scott No. 76), which went from 85 cents to $13.50 in a decade.

INDIA

India, another part of the British Commonwealth, is a vast, confusing field that is better left to specialists, if your motives are purely for investment. There are early stamps used in British India during the nineteenth century up through 1947 when partition divided the territory into India and Pakistan, stamps of modern India, and those of numerous feudatory states over which Britain exercised little internal control. The market for all of these is likely to be much stronger in Great Britain than it is in the United States. However, some have tripled in *Scott Catalogue* value in the past decade. Among the modern items, I refer you to the dramatic 10-rupee Gandhi Profile of 1948 (Scott No. 206), which rose from $6 to $25 in a decade.

Most nations of Western Europe maintain strong philatelic markets, and the earlier issues of the Communist bloc countries are also attractive for investors.

AUSTRIA

Austria was one of the first European nations to issue stamps, beginning with the period of the Austrian monarchy in 1850. The 3-kreuzer red Franz Joseph portrait of 1850 (Scott No. 3) was $75 in 1964 and had soared to $160 a decade later. In that same early set, the 9-kreuzer blue (Scott No. 5) went from $110 to $300 during the same period.

A 1955 set of five stamps to mark the tenth anniversary of Austria's liberation from Nazi Germany (Scott Nos. 599-603) has gone from $4.60 to $26.40 in a decade and was recently retailing for up to $20 in never-hinged condition. A 1956 issue to mark the 200th anniversary of the birth of Mozart (Scott No. 609) has moved from 90 cents to $3, partly because so many philatelists collect by a topic, such as music or composers.

EARLY BELGIUM IS "MONEY IN THE BANK"

Belgium's early sets, well-centered and never-hinged, are "money in the bank," according to some investment specialists. For example, the 1-franc greenish-brown King Leopold II of 1884 (Scott No. 54) has moved from $30 to $115 in ten years. The 2-franc King Albert I of 1912 (Scott No. 101) went from $1.75 to $6, and the high value of that set, the 5-franc plum-colored King Albert (Scott No. 102), is up from $7 to $32.50.

For big spenders, there is an inverted error of the 1920 65-centime claret and black Town Hall of Termonde (Scott No. 139a), which was going for $1,350 a decade ago and has since soared to above $4,000. At a more modest level, a 5-franc red-brown souvenir sheet of four, to mark the 1924 International Philatelic Exhibition at Brussels (# 171), has gone from $8 to $30.

INVESTMENT FAVORITES FROM FRANCE

The stamps of France are frequently distinguished by gorgeous designs, although the highest-priced items appear quite drab. Here is a sampling of possibles that spans several decades:

| | Catalogue Value | |
Description/Date/Scott No.	1964	1974
1-franc dull-orange-red Ceres, 1849 (#8a) .... $	1,500.0	$10,000.00
2-franc orange & pale-blue Le Havre Exhibition, 1929 (#246)	70.00	175.00
5-franc carmine Philatelic Exhibition souvenir sheet, 1925 (#226)	47.50	200.00
Two souvenir sheets from the Strasbourg Exhibition, 1927 (#241)	80.00	250.00
1-franc claret & olive-green Philatelic Congress of Bordeaux overprint, 1923 (#1971)	32.50	135.00

FINLAND

Traveling northward, we find that Finland's first stamp, the 5-kopeck blue Coat of Arms of 1856, went from $750 to $2,400 in a decade. In 1930, that country issued a 10-markka gray-lilac landscape of Lake Saima (Scott No. 178), which in ten years went from $10 to $30.

MAJOR OPPORTUNITIES FROM GERMANY

With the possible exception of England, West Germany may be Europe's strongest philatelic market. Its economy is solid, and its collectors sustain a high demand for classic material, as well as issues immediately following World War II. Some collectors even specialize in World War I forgeries issued by British propagandists, and pay high prices for these counterfeit items.

Here is a brief review of some German material, spanning nearly a century:

	Catalogue Value	
Description/Date/Scott No.	*1964*	*1974*
½-groschen red-orange Imperial Eagle of 1872 (#3)	$80.00	$265.00
18-kreuzer bistre Imperial Eagle of 1872 (#11) ...	75.00	240.00
80-pfennig lake & black Germania, 1900 (#61) ...	9.50	30.00
30-pfennig blue W.K. Roentgen, 1951 (#686)	5.50	20.00
5-pfennig Mona Lisa, 1952 (#687)	.15	1.50
1959 souvenir sheet of German composers (#804)..	3.00	13.50

Some of the German "dead states" are also attractive for investment. Prussia, a former kingdom in northern Germany, issued stamps from 1850-1867. The 2-silbergroschen blue profile of King Frederick, issued in 1857 (Scott No. 7), went from $275 to $1,000 in the past decade.

See, also, the stamps of Schleswig-Holstein, a former duchy in North Germany, which issued stamps from 1850 to 1866. The 1-schilling dull-blue Coat of Arms of 1850 (Scott No. 1) has gone from $50 to $200. Another little-known area for collectors is Thurn and Taxis, a princely house which issued its own stamps (1852-1867) prior to being incorporated into the German Empire. Its 2-silbergroschen yellow stamp of 1852 (Scott No. 7) went from $35 to $275 in a decade.

Another interesting "dead state" is Lombardy-Venetia, formerly a kingdom in northern Italy that was part of the Austrian Empire. These stamps were issued between 1850 and 1865. The 10-centesimi black Coat of Arms of 1850 (Scott No. 3) has gone from $175 to $600. The 10-soldi blue of 1863 (Scott No. 18) has gone from $300 to $1,000.

EVEN ANDORRA IS PROFITABLE

Also tiny, but far from dead, is the 191-square mile principality of Andorra, which is subject to the joint control of France and the Spanish Bishop of Urgel, and therefore uses both Spanish pesetas and French francs as currency. Andorra earns much of its revenue from the sale of its postage stamps.

The first set issued under French administration in 1931 (Scott Nos. 1-22) excites strong demand; the high value of the set, the 20-franc magenta and green (Scott No. 22), went from $18.50 in 1964 to $65 in 1974. A Spanish administration stamp of 1928, the 10-peseta brown with black overprint (Scott No. 12), was $13.50 and went to $40, but beware of counterfeit overprints.

One can go on and on through the nations of Western Europe, but I think I have made amply clear that there are numerous options. Switzerland is another excellent choice, because of its attractive stamps and solid economy. See especially the *Pro Juventute* stamps issued prior to 1939—"Buy, don't sell," says one investment counselor. Ditto for many items from Scandinavia, the Netherlands, Italy, and tiny areas such as San Marino, Luxembourg, Liechtenstein and the Vatican.

The investment prospects are less rosy in Spain and Portugal. Compare their standards of living with those of Switzerland and Germany, for example, and you'll see why the local economies support no sturdy stamp markets in Madrid or Lisbon.

EASTERN EUROPE: BOON AND BANE

The nations of Eastern Europe, the so-called "Communist Bloc," are problematic for the investor. There is no question that nineteenth-century material from Russia, Poland, Hungary, Yugoslavia, etc., is scarce and in demand.

But in the past decade or two, some of these nations have issued far too many stamps in large quantities, thus cheapening the general image of their national philatelic output. Also, political hostility by many Americans toward these nations has tended to depress the market here. But, as we move from a period of cold war to détente, one also detects a thaw in the philatelic market.

Wholesalers in the United States advertise recent Russian stamps for only 20 to 25 percent of *Scott Catalogue* value. But many pre-1960 Russian items are moving upward. At a recent auction, an old 1872 Russian cover mailed to Palestine was assigned an estimated value of $250 to $350, but the opening bid was $1,500 and it sold for $6,250.

One senses that there are many bargains nestled in the mountain of cheap material released by these nations in the past three decades. But beware of speculation, or you'll be seriously burned. As always, don't invest unless you've carefully analyzed actual market values, as opposed to catalogue values.

Numerous issues of Hungary's classical period, for example, are appreciating in price, as are a handful of more recent items.

In 1951, Hungary issued a 60-forint olive-green stamp to mark the eightieth anniversary of its first postage stamp (Scott No. 973). While many other stamps of that same period are virtually worthless, this one has climbed from 25 cents to $1.35 in a decade. The topic (designs of old stamps depicted on new stamps, known as "stamps on stamps") was of great interest to many collectors, and only 60,000 were issued. At the same time, Hungary released only 15,000 airmail souvenir sheets of a similar 80th Anniversary Design (Scott No. C95), and the price for this attractive item rose in a decade from $2.50 to $8.50.

ASIA, AFRICA AND THE MIDDLE EAST

The specialist can likely profit from the stamps of any area, but issues of Asia, Africa and the Middle East can be dangerous for the beginner. In general, the better materials come from the old colonies of these areas. Nations that have emerged since World War II are much less reliable in terms of investment. Their stamps are relatively new and hard to chart.

Early China has very scarce material that is worth investigation. The Republic of China (Taiwan) began to issue stamps in

1949 and some of its early sets are climbing at a rate of 10 to 20 percent yearly. Since the United States resumed relations with The People's Republic of China ("Red China" to cold warriors), there has been renewed interest. In fact, until recently it was illegal to purchase stamps of The People's Republic.

You might check on the three-stamp Asiatic Congress set of 1949 (Scott Nos. 5-7), which went from $1.35 to $2.25 in a single year, or the Picasso Dove of Peace design of 1950 (Scott Nos. 57-59) that soared from $1.90 to $8, or Lin Piao's Epigram on Mao Tse-Tung of 1967 (Scott No. 981), or Mao Tse-Tung Going to An Yuan of 1968 (Scott No. 998), all of which are rising in value.

Japan, with an industrialized society and large middle class, has a strong stamp market. South Korea, too, has shown upward price movement. See, for example, the souvenir sheet of 1956, printed in tiny quantities to mark the Melbourne Olympic Games.

ISRAEL: A MAJOR MARKET FOR INVESTORS

The beleaguered Republic of Israel is an unusual case. Not only is the demand for stamps strong locally, its stamps also generate great interest in the United States and other parts of the diaspora. Chauvinism, however, is not the only reason. Israel has pursued a conservative postal policy, issuing stamps in moderate quantities and featuring exquisite designs, often with Biblical themes that have widespread appeal.

The strongest values are the stamps issued during the five years following Israel's independence in 1948. I refer particularly to the Ancient Judean Coins of 1948 (Scott Nos. 1-9), the first airmails (Scott Nos. C1-C6) and the first Postage Due stamps of 1948 (Scott Nos. J1–J5).

There is a unique aspect to collecting stamps from Israel. Its stamps are printed with tabs that are connected to stamps along the bottom row of each sheet. Since only the bottom row of each sheet has tabs, stamps with tabs are rarer and normally sell for 25 to 50 percent more. In some cases, the difference is far more dramatic. For example, the Judean Coins of 1948 recently whole-saled for $14 a set without tabs. The same set with tabs cost $230! The early airmails were offered for $20, but cost ten times that amount when they had tabs attached.

Some of the more recent material has also gone up quickly. In two years, the 1-pound S.S. Shalom of 1963 (Scott No. 250) soared in value in Europe from $3 to $15. Another good bet is the Holy Arks set of 1972 (Scott Nos. 497–500). A tab set went up from $1.10 to $3.80 in two years. Check also the 1952 Menorah stamp (Scott No. 55). In 1974, it was $185 with tabs; only a few months later it was wholesaling for $225.

I happen to collect Israel stamps, so I have a few personal experiences to relate. In 1972, I bought a small quantity of a new commemorative called Let My People Go (Scott No. 487). The text was inscribed in Hebrew, Arabic, Russian and English. It was an obvious reference to the controversial issue of Jewish emigration from Russia. Topical interest was inevitable. A min-iature sheet of fifteen of these stamps had a post-office face value of $1.98. The five tab stamps along the bottom had a face value of 13 cents apiece. This year, the full sheet was selling for about $27, and each tab stamp was being offered for over $4.

I felt like kicking myself for not buying more. But even many dealers were caught unprepared, because they began to advertise heavily in an effort to acquire material for their clients. Their strong advertising also spurred demand and moved the price steadily upward.

At the same time, much of Israel's recent material is not necessarily a good investment. Some dealers have very ample supplies, and you would have a hard time reselling it. Also, Israel's currency was devalued by 42 percent in early 1975, which depressed the worth of current material.

I believe that Israel's early stamps are still a very good in-vestment bet. Also, even some recent miniature sheets of fifteen are worth acquiring, providing you are very selective and don't go overboard. The very recent set of stamps honoring David Ben-Gurion, for example, appears to have evoked strong response from collectors. A sheet of these cost $5.58 at face value, and recent retail ads have been asking $20.*

There are many places to buy Israel material. In fact, if you qualify as a dealer, you can purchase new issues at face value from the Israel Philatelic Agency in America, 515 Sixth Avenue, New York, N.Y. 10036. The minimum order is $15. For older material, you'll find numerous "buy" and "sell" ads in stamp periodicals.

THE RISKS OF LATIN AMERICA

Market values of Latin American stamps offer a perfect example of the rule that "a stamp's basic demand is generated in its home country." Since most Latin American nations are part of the Third World and struggle along with relatively backward economies, their stamps are subject to heavy discounts from the *Scott Catalogue* value, and few of them appear to be profitable investments.

This is true even though many are issued in minuscule quantities. As I mentioned before, scarcity is of little import if you don't have customers. For example, a Guatemala airmail set of 1931 (Scott Nos. C17–C19) that marks the first flights to Miami was issued in a quantity of only 10,000. But the catalogue value has held steady at $13.50 for years.

---

* Major currency fluctuations affect the stamp market just as they have impact upon the value of other commodities. For example, when German and Swiss currencies were revalued upward, this doubled the prices of cheese and chocolates imported to the United States from those areas. The value of German and Swiss stamps and of other stamps sold in those countries also experienced rises. Some stamp dealers are quite expert in the international sale and purchase of stamps, profiting from the differences in currency values between nations. This type of activity is known as "arbitrage." Unless you are fully familiar with stamps as well as the intricacies of international currency exchange, don't tinker with it. But, as mentioned earlier, some of the "better" countries for stamp investment are those with strong economies and solid currencies.

A 5-centavo stamp of 1904 from the Dominican Republic (Scott No. 159) is said to exist in a quantity of only 100, exactly the same number as the U.S. Jenny Invert that recently sold for $47,000. However, this equally scarce Dominican stamp has a catalogue value of only $200.

But Latin America may be a philatelic sleeper area. There has been an upsurge of interest in Europe. In late 1974 at a Stanley Gibbons auction in London, sixty-four lots of South American material brought about 30 percent above the estimated value. A proof of the Guatemalan inverted center of 1881 (Scott No. 22), for example, which catalogued for only $75, was sold for $230 at this auction.

The overall "image" of Latin American material is still damaged by the practices of a few countries that issue totally unnecessary material. Nicaragua, for example, recently issued a high-priced homage to Winston Churchill (seven stamps and two souvenir sheets), even though this great statesman is irrelevant to that country's history. This issue may enrich the Nicaraguan treasury to some extent, but as an investment its value is quite dubious.

ARE TREASURES BURIED IN BRAZIL?

Yet the stamps of a giant nation such as Brazil are available at quite modest levels. An article in *Linn's Weekly* predicted:

> Brazil seems to have everything going for it—ample resources, growing industry, a growing middle class. [Brazil] will almost certainly move into the circle of great powers. When this happens, Brazilian stamps may turn into very good items, indeed.

One specialist recommends a 1900 set (Scott Nos. 162–165) that marks the fourth centenary of Brazil's discovery. Only 100,000 sets were issued. Perhaps he has inside information, but I hesitate to recommend this set, because in the past ten years its catalogue value has gone up only from $5 to $7. As you know, I prefer stamps that already have a clear upward trajectory: For example, the 3,000-reis violet airmail of 1937 (Scott No. C38) moved from $2.75 to $11 in a decade. The 100-reis red stamp of 1908 (Scott No. 190), which marks the opening of Brazilian ports to foreign commerce, has gone up from 25 cents to $3 in a decade. The 300-reis olive-gray Mercury of 1920 (Scott No. 228), which is the key stamp in a popular set, has moved from 40 cents to $2.25 in the same span of time. Multiple quantities of these could be a profitable speculative investment.

Other South American nations with fairly strong economies are oil-rich Venezuela and Argentina, which has a large, literate middle class.

CUBA

Cuba has been another victim of the cold war. Because of U.S. interest in this Caribbean republic since the turn of the century, many Americans collected its stamps and supported a healthy philatelic market. But in 1962, President Kennedy prohibited the import of all Cuban stamps. Since then, it has only been legal to buy or sell pre-Castro stamps that already were in this country. This policy is inconsistent, because we are allowed to import the stamps of such Communist giants as Russia and China.

Of course, the rest of the world pays no attention to the U.S. embargo on Cuba, and there is a lively market for its stamps, new and old, in Canada, England, Spain, and elsewhere. If, as I suspect, we reach détente with the Caribbean republic, the value of Cuban stamps could well spurt upward.

Some of the nineteenth-century Cuban material moves up with or without détente. Consider the 40-centavo rose Queen Isabella II of 1866 (Scott No. 26), up from $1 to $3 in a decade.

I also like a 1939 airmail (Scott No. C31), issued in connection with an experimental postal rocket flight held at Havana. Only about 200,000 were issued. Its price went from $8 in 1964 to $25 in 1974. A mint copy was recently wholesaling for $12 and retailing for about $20. Many topical collectors who specialize in "space" stamps boost the market for this item.

Most volatile are the stamps issued in the early days of the Castro revolution, shortly before the U.S. embargo. Take a set of 1956–59 stamps that were surcharged with new values in 1960 (Scott Nos. 629–636). One of these, the 2-centavo on 14-centavo gray (Scott No. 636), has gone up from a nickel to 18 cents in a decade. If you had several sheets of this one, you would possess a promising item.

A 1960 airmail (Scott No. C214), marking the thirtieth anniversary of Cuban airmail service, has gone from 60 cents to $2.25. A possible sleeper is the 1961 Jose Martí and the Declaration of Havana souvenir sheet of three (Scott Nos. C219–C221), which has only gone up from $1.25 to $2 in a decade. But its subject has historical significance and it might increase in value. Of course, I prefer to wait until it begins to climb and then invest.

If you want to keep current on the market for Cuban stamps without illegally purchasing Castro-era material, you can request the quarterly magazine *Filatelia Cubana,* published by the Ecofil Philatelic Agency, 54 Conduit Street, London W1, England. For earlier material, there are several Cuban philatelic clubs on the U.S. mainland.

Let me sum up this section with a few suggestions. Unless you have limitless time, and a computerlike memory, you would do well to restrict your interests to a single country or two at most. It can take years to become expert in the stamps of a major country, so you will be diluting your knowledge if you spread yourself too thin.

Once you decide upon a country, become a *collector* of that country's stamps, even though your principal motive is investment. Only by becoming a collector can you acquire a proper feel for the market value of that country's stamps. Buy a specialized album of that country. Then purchase the largest collection of unused stamps of the country that you can afford. You can do so at great discount via an auction, or in some advertised special. This will enable you to fill up a fair portion of the blank spaces in your album.

At that point, begin to focus upon the good investment items and search them out, adding to your collection. In a few years or so, you'll have a good country-collection. You will probably enjoy the mere possession of it, and it will be worth something, too. Also, purchase multiple quantities of the better investment items whenever you can. Store these in a safe or in a bank safety deposit box. If you develop a personal affection for the album collection, as many people do, but wish to cash in on part of your holdings, you can always sell off the duplicates.

I think by now you have a fair idea of which countries are better, philatelically speaking, and why certain stamps appreciate more rapidly than others.

But this will be of no use to you unless you understand the price structure of the stamp world, and the influence of a stamp's condition upon its market value. The next chapter deals with these essentials.

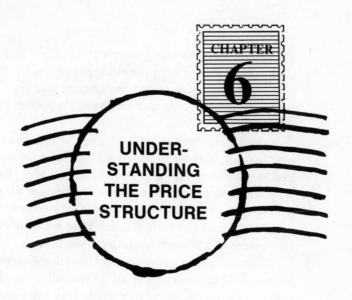

CHAPTER

6

UNDER-
STANDING
THE PRICE
STRUCTURE

Once you decide which stamps have promising investment potential, you naturally want to acquire them at a proper price, and we have already seen that the stamp price structure can be confusing to the newcomer.

Let's start at the beginning of the process, to see how the value of a new stamp is established.

In early 1975, a 10-cent commemorative stamp is issued by the U.S. Postal Service in a quantity of 150 million. For several weeks, the stamp is available at any post office for 10 cents. Then it is taken off sale, but large supplies have been purchased by wholesalers, for future stamp collectors. A few retailers have also bought modest amounts to serve near-future needs, but they won't tie up too much of their capital in such items.

The next edition of the *Scott Catalogue* will normally assign a value of 20 cents to that 10-cent stamp, double the face value.

This will become the widely accepted "top retail" price, and most dealers will sell it for a few pennies less, a discount from Scott but still a few pennies more than the original face value. After all, they must make a profit, and reimburse themselves for handling costs.

Since this stamp is quite common, a block of four joined together will probably be assigned a catalogue value of 80 cents, exactly four times the value of a single stamp. A plate block of four will catalogue at a slight premium, perhaps $1, or 25 cents per stamp, because not every group of four stamps on the sheet is located adjacent to a plate number. Here we begin to introduce the concept of scarcity in a stamp's price structure.

Since the stamp is common and abundant, it is unlikely that its price will rise much, if at all. There will always be a ready supply for collectors. As years pass, its price will remain roughly the same, with slow gains due to inflation. But its value will be closely tied to its original face value.

This is the case for most stamps issued since the 1940s. For example, the 3-cent violet American Eagle of 1942 (Scott No. 905) started out as a 6-cent catalogue item (double its face value) and, only due to inflation, has inched up to 10 cents today. The same is true of a 1967 5-cent Christmas stamp (Scott No. 1336), which was first assigned a catalogue value of 10 cents. Now, with inflation, it catalogues at 12 cents. This is hardly a good investment.

If for some reason the demand for a certain stamp far exceeds its actual supply, it will shoot up quickly in value, at a rate faster than inflation. Soon, its market value will have little or no relation to its face value. It has, in a sense, taken off.

Even today some very old U.S. stamps have not yet taken off, and it is unlikely that they ever will. Let's take the case of a 2-cent green stamp issued in 1887 (Scott No. 213). It is nearly ninety years old, yet it can still be purchased for about $2. Why? Because it was issued in a quantity of 3.5 billion. That's an excellent reason why. Millions of these stamps are still floating around in unused condition.

CONDITION AS A PRICE FACTOR

Although the *Scott Catalogue* price of a stamp is a good barometer for its year-to-year fluctuations in value, you are treading on very dangerous ground if you blindly adhere to the catalogue value when you purchase the stamp. A stamp's condition is perhaps the key determinant of its actual market value. You may see two advertisements that offer what is apparently the same stamp, yet one will cost twice as much as the other. Unless the condition of each stamp is clearly and correctly stated, there is no way to compare their relative values. You will also have to learn the difference between catalogue value, retail value, and wholesale value. Let's tackle these problems one at a time.

Since facts and figures speak louder than generalities, let's take the specific case of the U.S. Trans-Mississippi Exposition Issue of 1898. This includes nine stamps (Scott Nos. 285–293). The following table will list the stamps, show their *Scott Catalogue* values for 1975 and the prices asked by a major retailer in early 1975, in varying conditions. Study the table carefully:

RETAIL PRICES FOR TRANS-MISSISSIPPI ISSUE OF 1898

Stamp/Scott No.	1975 Cat. Value	Fine–Average	Fine	Very Fine	Extra Fine
1¢ (#285)	$ 8.25	$3.50	$ 6.50	$12.00	$20.00
2¢ (#286)	7.25	3.50	6.50	12.00	20.00
3¢ (#287)	37.50	13.00	26.00	55.00	70.00
5¢ (#288)	33.50	-	25.00	55.00	70.00
8¢ (#289)	47.50	15.00	38.00	75.00	95.00
10¢ (#290)	60.00	-	43.00	75.00	120.00
50¢ (#291)	225.00	-	165.00	350.00	600.00
$1 (#292)	500.00	285.00	360.00	450.00	800.00
$2 (#293)	725.00	305.00	575.00	1,100.00	1,500.00

The first thing you should note from this table is that in *no* case is a stamp being offered for its exact catalogue value. Does this mean that catalogue value is really not a general price barometer, after all, but really a worthless yardstick of a stamp's value?

Definitely not. If you look closer, you will see that virtually every price has a *relationship* to catalogue value.

Stamps in Extra Fine condition are retailing for sometimes more than double the catalogue value in the specific case of this attractive set of classics. Those in Very Fine condition are invariably well above the catalogue price. The condition that appears closest to catalogue value is Fine, and stamps of this category are usually offered for a shade below catalogue. Don't even consider buying anything less than Fine; I listed the princes for Fine–Average only to demonstrate as clearly as possible how huge a discount from catalogue value you can obtain for stamps in this less desirable condition.

As for myself, I stick to those in Fine or Very Fine condition, which, in the long run, may prove to be more stable investments. It has always been normal to pay above catalogue for Extra Fine and, in some cases, Very Fine, but I think that these premiums are frequently exorbitant, and reflect a great deal of demand being generated by non-philatelic money that is being poured into stamps from a troubled stock market.

Now, let's examine the same set of stamps in a different way. Trans-Mississippi stamps are frequently available at auction, where collectors compete with dealers for the same material. The following chart shows a few of these stamps, their 1974 *Scott Catalogue* value, and the prices most frequently paid that year for stamps in Fine and Very Fine condition:

AUCTION PRICES FOR TRANS-MISSISSIPPI ISSUE OF 1898

Stamp/Scott No.	1974 Cat. Val.	Fine	Very Fine
4¢ (#287)	$ 28.50	$ 19.00	$ 36.00
5¢ (#288)	26.00	19.00	35.00
8¢ (#289)	35.00	30.00	45.00
10¢ (#290)	47.50	40.00	65.00
50¢ (#291)	175.00	130.00	210.00
$1 (#292)	400.00	280.00	400.00
$2 (#293)	600.00	440.00	600.00

This comparison, I think, offers an intriguing lesson. First of all, we see a substantial difference between prices for Fine and Very Fine stamps. In the case of auctions, the Fine specimens invariably sold for below *Scott Catalogue* levels; the Very Fine often sold for above the Scott, and in a few cases for amounts identical to the Scott value.

Secondly, if you compare this table with the previous, you will see that the stamps could usually be purchased more cheaply at auction than in response to a retail advertisement. For example, a Fine copy of the $1 Trans-Mississippi was commonly obtained for $280 at auction, while the retail ad charged $360. The difference between auction price and retail price is the commission earned by the retailer. Of course, when you order from a retailer, you are virtually assured of getting your stamp. When you bid at auction, you are competing against many buyers, possibly including the retailer. (We'll discuss various modes of buying later on.)

Let's look again at the question of condition and its impact upon price. Another set of U.S. stamps which represents a better-than-average investment opportunity is the Panama-Pacific Exposition of 1913. The following table shows the 1975 *Scott*

Catalogue value for each stamp in the set and retail prices for these stamps in three types of condition.

RETAIL PRICES FOR PANAMA-PACIFIC EXPOSITION

Stamp/Scott No.	1975 Cat. Val.	Fine	Very Fine	Superb
1¢ (#397)	$ 5.00	$ 4.00	$ 6.50	$12.50
2¢ (#398)	5.50	4.75	7.50	14.00
5¢ (#399)	27.50	22.00	35.00	57.50
10¢ (#400)	50.00	48.50	65.00	100.00

Again we see that Superb copies sell for double or more than double the *Scott Catalogue* value, Very Fine are slightly above, and Fine are slightly below. This pattern applies only to better U.S. material, from the nineteenth and early twentieth century; price structures differ for other countries, and even for U.S. stamps of recent years, which frequently sell for under the *Scott Catalogue* value, even when they are in Very Fine condition.

As with the previous set, you can usually do better at auction, although there is no guarantee that you will get your stamp. In 1974, the 5-cent value of this set (Scott No. 399) was commonly sold at auction for $25 in Very Fine condition, as opposed to the $35 retail price. I might add, however, that anything goes at an auction. In some auctions, bids ranged as high as $48—and as low as $18—for the same stamp.

In the case of the 10-cent yellow (Scott No. 400), while a Very Fine retail price was $65, the average winning bid at auction was $50, with bids swinging as low as $34 and as high as $72.50.

As you can see, there is no simple rule. It takes constant comparisons of retail ads and auction results to keep abreast. I got these retail prices from ads in *Linn's Weekly*. I regularly clip them, file them away and use them for reference. You can devise a simple system to do the same. Just store them in a file folder under

"U.S. Retail," and refer to them when you contemplate a purchase.

HOW TO EVALUATE CONDITION

Judging the precise condition of a rare stamp is somewhat like wine or tea-tasting; it's a job for an expert, requiring a number of arbitrary decisions. But if you follow a few simple rules, you will be able to easily discern the difference between a Fine and a Superb stamp, or to identify a stamp that doesn't measure up to the Fine category.

One of the best treatises on this subject is a twenty-page booklet called *Evaluating the Condition of Postage Stamps,* by Harry V. Wood. [Write to H.V. Wood Co., PO Box 2295, Seal Beach, Cal. 90740]. Any beginner can follow it, and acquire substantial knowledge.

In the meantime, here are some key pointers:

1. When you examine a stamp, sit at a table or desk where the lighting is good. Take your time. Use stamp tongs to hold the stamp. Until you become quite expert, refer to your *Scott Catalogue* to confirm that the stamp is properly identified, and that its price bears proper correspondence to the catalogue value. I mention this, because certain U.S. stamps are quite similar in appearance, differing only in their perforation measurements or design details, but their values vary considerably. Observe the stamp through a magnifying glass. With a bit of patience, you will be surprised at the number of flaws that you can detect.

2. Don't even bother buying a stamp that is not intact, meaning that it is torn, has a serious thin, a pinhole, a missing perforation tooth, a visible crease, or is very faded or smudged.

3. Assuming that the stamp is intact, a substantial part of its value will be determined by how well it is centered. With

few exceptions, a stamp cannot be graded as Fine unless its design is clear of the perforations, that is, the perforations should not cut in to the design.

4. Check the stamp for thins in the paper, which can seriously affect its value. A major thin can be spotted immediately on the reverse side of the stamp, where some of the gum and paper will be visibly missing. A simple way to check for a thin is to hold the stamp up to a strong light, with its design facing you. If there is a thin, that part of the design will shine noticeably brighter. If so, the stamp is defective.

5. Now, concentrate on the reverse side of the stamp. Examine the condition of the gum. (Your catalogue will tell you that a few older stamps were issued without gum.) If there are no hinge marks, it could be described as never hinged. See whether the gum is badly cracked from age. If the stamp has a minor trace of a hinge, it would be described as lightly hinged. If there is a large hinge mark, but most of the original gum remains on the back of the stamp, it is usually described as original gum, or OG. If the stamp was originally issued with gum but has none, it would be considered unused. We are, of course, discussing a stamp that has not seen postal use.

6. Turn back to the face of the stamp and look for brightness of color, crisp details, cleanliness. Check the catalogue for the description of the stamp's color and confirm this. An inexpensive color guide can be purchased for this test. If there is a noticeable difference in color, you may well have a different variety of the stamp, which might vary a great deal in market value.

With a bit of practice, you can evaluate the condition of a stamp in a couple of minutes. You will certainly be able to spot major flaws.

HOW TO JUDGE HINGING AS PART OF CONDITION

As long as the back of a stamp is in reasonably good condition, I personally couldn't care whether it is never-hinged or lightly-hinged. But a never-hinged mania has spread among many philatelists, causing the price of these stamps to be greatly inflated.

This is a fairly recent phenomenon. Many years ago, some collectors even used the gum of their uncancelled stamps to affix them to the album pages. Later, it was common to affix a never-hinged stamp to the album with a paper hinge. Until the 1920s, hingeless stamp mounts were not available. Back in 1922, an article in a stamp journal noted that "some want OG, some don't." It mentioned that many nineteenth-century collectors preferred no gum at all on their stamps because "OG often had a detrimental influence." Age sometimes caused the gum to turn a dark brown, also discoloring the stamp. Insects ate the gum off the paper, causing tiny blotches. Gum grew brittle and cracked, sometimes cracking the paper, too. Humidity caused stamps to stick to album pages.

But the OG mania has continued to grow. Many stamps are now surreptitiously regummed, and their prices are jacked up correspondingly. This is a reality that must be faced. As a rough guideline to the cost of never-hinged stamps, here's what the Stanley Gibbons Company says in its recent retail price list for U.S. stamps:

> Mint [i.e. unhinged] stamps of the earlier issues are difficult to locate and it is therefore necessary to make an extra charge for them. This charge is: issues prior to 1920—25%; from 1920 to 1929—20%; and from 1930 to 1950—10%. Issues after 1950 can generally be supplied in mint condition without extra charge, upon request.

I advise you not to pay a huge premium for never-hinged stamps, and if you do pay any premium at all, not to exceed the guidelines established by Gibbons.

Talking about premiums, collectors are paying what I regard to be exorbitant prices for stamps described by some auction galleries as having "jumbo" or "boardwalk" margins, meaning that the margins framing the design are unusually large, and very well centered. I wholeheartedly agree with Herman Herst, Jr., who wrote recently that it is better to have two Very Fine $5 Columbian stamps at $1,800 (their catalogue value) than one "jumbo superb" of the same stamp at $1,800. As he observes, it will be easier later to find two people who appreciate fine stamps, than one "perfection crank" who has a passion for "jumbos."

While I suspect that much of this premium money being poured into top quality stamps does come from non-philatelic sources (i.e., escapees from the crumbling stock market), Mr. Herst says:

> The sad fact is that a substantial part of the money being poured into stamps today will never be returned to the buyer when they try to sell, and the equally sad corollary is that these are the people who got into stamps primarily to make money.

CATALOGUE PRICES

While there is no universal price for a particular stamp at a given time, even a stamp's "Scott value" leaves you in the dark because it does not constitute a real asking price.

To determine these real asking prices, you must consult a variety of sources. Many dealers publish price lists as advertisements in the stamp press. Some very large dealers such as Stanley Gibbons and Harris publish annual price lists that are like small catalogues in scope. I've mentioned the Brookman Company of

South Orange, N.J., whose miniature catalogue is used as a price list by hundreds of small and medium-sized retailers. Some of these price lists—the Gibbons, for instance—are net prices, while others will allow discounts from them. Many dealers who use the Brookman list, for example, will offer you a discount from the published price.

To get an idea of how these price tags compare, let's look at a particular stamp. In order to make a valid comparison, always be sure that any stamp that is being offered by each source is in similar condition.

$1 Columbian of 1893, Fine, unused

1975 *Scott Catalogue*	$350.00
Stanley Gibbons	293.00
Brookman	350.00
Retail ad in *Linn's Weekly*	265.00
Another retail ad in *Linn's Weekly*	175.00

As you can see, there are great differences. You can be sure that each advertiser claims that his stamp is in Fine condition, although you cannot be sure until you see it. In some cases, a stamp may be offered at a very low price because the dealer made a very fortunate purchase, is well-stocked, and can make a handsome profit even by offering bargain rates. The same dealer may not offer consistently low prices for all items. This is why it is important to compare. You would normally do some comparison shopping when you plan to buy a car, a major appliance, or even certain grocery items. The same principle should hold true for stamps that involve expenditures of hundreds of dollars or more. I find this footwork to be fun, and unless you're rich there is no sensible alternative.

"BUY" PRICE AS A FACTOR IN SALES PRICE

If you plan a major purchase, it would also be a good idea to examine the "buy" offers of stamp dealers. Again, the "buy" price varies from dealer to dealer, depending upon his inventory needs. Many small dealers use the Harris Company's published list of top buying prices as a guide, although this tends to be on the low side, since it uses as its criteria stamps that are in Good condition before 1890 and Fine after 1890.

In the case of the $1 Columbian we've just compared, Harris offers to buy it for $145. Another large dealer offers $162.50. Still another offers $260, providing it is never-hinged. Another claims it will pay $325 for Very Fine and lightly-hinged. As you can see, there is also quite a variety here, too, and it must be checked out from case to case.

If this sounds chaotic, be consoled by the fact that no one in the world of philately—including dealers—has access to inside information as is the case on the stock market. Most stamp transactions are public. If you do your homework, taking note of the many buy and sell ads that appear in the press, you will be as well informed as many dealers.

For example, you can learn something by comparing the Harris Company's top buying prices and the prices it asks for certain stamps in its retail catalogue. Here are examples of four recent U.S. plate blocks:

Description/ Date/ Scott No.	Harris "Sell"	Harris "Buy"
1¼¢ light-green, Gallatin, 1967 (#1279)	$ 15.95	$ 7.80
80¢ Hawaii, 1952 airmail (#C46)	48.75	22.75
10¢ Curtiss Jenny 1968 airmail (#C74)	13.95	6.00
10¢ Man on the Moon, 1969 airmail (#C76)	3.25	1.00

Harris's "buy" prices tend to be on the low side, but their ratio of buy/sell is instructive. For three of the four stamps shown above, the "buy" price is roughly one-half of the "sell" price. But the "buy" price for the 10-cent Man on the Moon airmail is only about one-third of the "sell" price, meaning that Harris has a fairly abundant supply of this item and is hardly desperate to acquire it. This says something about the stamp's scarcity, and indicates that its retail "sell" price may be much too high.

You'll see frequent examples of such "buy/sell" data in the stamp press, and it's worth examining. Here, for example, is part of the text of a recent ad in *Linn's Weekly,* with "buy" and "sell" prices for full mint sheets of United Nations stamps.

Stamp/ Scott No.	Buy per sheet	Sell per sheet
1951 first set (#1–11)	$450.00	$600.00
1953 UPU (#17–18)	120.00	160.00
1953 Technical Assistance (#19–20) .	55.00	80.00
1955 Human Rights (#39-40)	30.00	45.00

Note that the dealer will sell the first set at a 33⅓ percent markup above his "buy" price, and the same for the UPU set. However, in the case of the next two sets, he is marking them up by about 50 percent. Why? One cannot be certain. But the fact that there is a very large gap between "buy" and "sell" probably indicates that he is well-stocked with this item, or can easily acquire it. Therefore, $45 may be too much to pay for a set that he will buy back for only $30. If he can get it cheaper, so can you, with a little effort.

HOW TO USE PRICES REALIZED

There is no substitute for empirical data when you plan to purchase stamps. Prices realized at auctions give you the actual market value of a given stamp at a given place and time.

Not long ago, Frank L. Sente, the librarian of the American Philatelic Research Library, wrote: "I firmly believe that a ten-year run of auction catalogues from a major auction gallery with prices realized contains more information than a library of price catalogues, handbooks and journals occupying the same amount of shelf space."

Most major auction galleries publish a list of these "prices realized" at the conclusion of each sale. These are usually available for a nominal charge. In fact, you can subscribe on an annual basis to receive the auction catalogues and lists of prices realized of some galleries.

When the time comes for you to purchase a particular stamp, either from a retailer or at auction, check over the lists of prices realized to see what it has been selling for at auction. Another invaluable source of information (I mentioned this previously, but it merits repeating) is *The Green Book of Stamps,* a compilation of prices realized from many galleries throughout the country published by APR Publishers, Inc., PO Box 889, Fresno, Cal. 93714. In its last edition, *The Green Book* included prices realized from 125 different auctions conducted by twenty major galleries.

It's interesting to note, by the way, that eleven of these galleries were located on the East Coast, two were in the Midwest and seven were on the West Coast. The publishers saw "no discernible difference" in the level of prices realized by geographical area.

To appreciate the value of prices-realized results, let's refer again to the $1 Columbian stamp of 1893. A few moments ago, we saw that its catalogue value was $350, and that retail offers to sell varied from a low of $175 up to $350 for a fine, unused copy. *The Green Book* shows that during 1974 such copies sold at auction for as low as $130 and as high as $300, while the median was $200. It sold for $200 on 19 different occasions.

The lesson is that $350 is too high a price to pay for this stamp. Getting it at $200 would constitute a good buy, and acquiring it for much less would be an exceptional buy.

On the other hand, we also know that knowledgeable collectors will gladly pay well above catalogue value for truly scarce material that is in superior condition. In a November 1974 auction, older U.S. stamps sold by the H.R. Harmer Gallery had a total catalogue value of $142,000. However, the prices realized added up to $151,187. While many of the stamps sold for well below the catalogue value, others drew bids that were close to double catalogue. In stamps, one man's bonanza may become another's bargain. It's up to you.

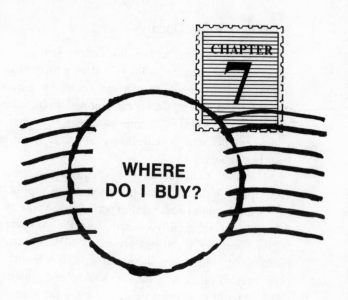

WHERE DO I BUY?

The moment of truth arrives. You have compiled a list of worthwhile stamp investments. You know something about the importance of a stamp's condition, and you have an idea of how to determine a fair market price for a given stamp. Now you face the dilemma: Where do I buy?

I advise you to develop a variety of sources.

If you have $1,000 or more to spend at a time, it will be worth the time of a large dealer to sell you a good accumulation purely for investment, and charge only a modest commission.

But don't forget your local retailer. Patronize his store for items such as catalogues, albums, and other accessories. Let him know that you are in the market for certain scarce stamps in Fine condition or better. Give him a list of the catalogue numbers of these stamps. This is known as a "want list."

131

You won't want to buy his stamps at high markup retail prices. But he may be willing to deal with you at a reduced commission. After all, he can earn more by acquiring a $500 stamp for you, at a modest commission, than by selling dozens of cheap stamp packets to juvenile hobbyists. If your time is limited, a local retailer who is both honest and competent may well be your best answer.

However, to be sure that he is acquiring your stamps for you at competitive prices, check other sources of supply.

Scan the retail ads in stamp periodicals. Write away for price lists that are frequently offered. Join the American Philatelic Society, and ask to be put on their "sales circuits." These are booklets of stamps circulated for sale, containing the surplus properties of other APS members. You can sometimes pick up good material at reasonable prices, since the stamps for sale in these circuits are members' duplicates that they wish to convert into cash.

If you decide to amass a collection of the stamps of a particular country, and wish to receive all future items issued by that country, you might subscribe to a new-issue service. You'll see several of these listed in stamp journals. For approximately 20 percent above the original face value, these services will send you all stamps issued by the country that you collect. With rare exceptions, as I have shown, new issues are not good investments, but if you get these items at slightly above post office value you can't go too far wrong, and you will keep your country collection as complete as possible.

BUYING NEW ISSUES DIRECTLY

You can also purchase new issues of most countries at face value directly from their post offices. This often involves purchasing international money orders, and will require you to engage in some correspondence. But the extra time and trouble can result in real savings if you purchase significant amounts, and there is always the added and intangible fun of receiving your material directly from the country. This may not be worth it if you buy only one of each new stamp being issued, to keep your country collection current. But let us suppose that you learn of a new stamp that will be issued, whose topic, design, and quantity make it quite attractive in terms of investment. I would not risk large amounts on such speculative material, but by purchasing a small quantity directly from the post office involved, you can add some spice to your portfolio. Unless the currency of the country involved is seriously devalued, you stand a good chance of getting all or most of your money back, even if the stamp does not rise in price as anticipated.

Auction catalogues are full of these "mistakes," and they usually sell for close to, or slightly above, face value. For a low-cost list of names and addresses of postal agencies all over the world, write to: Leonard I. Kindler, 3366 Red Lion Road, Philadelphia, Pa. 19114.

One final tip on new issues: Keep alert for low-quantity issues of overprinted stamps. If a country's political status changes, it will often overprint this information on its current stamps, while new stamps are being produced. If these overprints are in use for only a limited duration, they might become quite scarce.

A case in point is the 1960 Cyprus set of fifteen stamps (Scott Nos. 183–197). When this former British Crown Colony became a republic in 1960, previously existing stamps were overprinted in Greek and Turkish with the words "Republic of Cyprus." At the time, they were available for $8.95. Today, their catalogue value is $103.

Another occasion for overprinting comes when a nation changes its currency system, or raises the cost of its postage, and—while new stamps are being designed and printed—issues a limited supply of old stamps with new information. This occurred in 1967, when the Cook Islands' monetary unit was changed from the pound to the dollar; three stamps (Scott Nos. 192–194) were surcharged in red ink, with dollar values printed over the old pound values. A few months later, brand-new stamps were produced, using only the dollar values. Because they are so scarce, these three overprinted stamps, which were high values and cost $39.50 to start with, now have a catalogue value of $650.

SHOULD YOU USE INVESTMENT SERVICES?

You will see ads for investment services that offer to sell you stamps that they claim are going up in value or are likely to go up. I would like to warn you of possible pitfalls. Let me give you an example of why I entertain these doubts. I recently took a trial subscription to the services of one stamp investment broker who has been in the business for several years. I was impressed with his advertising approach. He made no wild claims. He urged caution and warned that in some cases "stamp prices go down as well as up." So I sent a first check for $25.

I must say that I was baffled by what he sent me. Part of my investment package consisted of 15 sets of 1954 Malta stamps (Scott Nos. 243–45). His price was quite reasonable, at a good discount from the *Scott Catalogue*. But were they a good investment? I noticed that in 1965, this set had a *Scott Catalogue* value of $1.12. Ten years later, their value was $1.70. A ten-year gain of 52 percent was hardly enough to keep up with inflation. My investment package was completed by six sets of a 1964 Cyprus set (Scott Nos. 247–250). Again, the selling price was reasonable. But this set was catalogued at $2.15 in 1969 and had crept up to only $2.35 in 1975, six years later. I couldn't for the life of me figure out why these stamps were likely to appreciate in price at a rate that constitutes a good investment.

I wrote to the man, expressing my doubts. I asked for my $25 back, enclosing the stamps in return, and said that I would be happy to resume my investing if he could provide me with some rationale to show that these Malta and Cyprus stamps would increase in value in the future.

The gentleman promptly refunded my $25 and took the trouble to write me a lengthy personal letter, explaining that both of these stamps had, in recent months, experienced sharp rises in value in European markets. I was impressed by his apparent honesty and sincerity, but his rationale gave me little incentive to continue investing through his brokerage service.

We *know* that certain nineteenth-century stamps have been rising at a steady clip for decade after decade. This, to me, is investment. But to expect that stamps issued in the 1950s and 1960s will go up markedly in value (even on the basis of inside information) is still speculation, I believe. Malta #243-45 and Cyprus #247-50 may someday take off and prove to be sterling investments. But why take such risks when safer options are available?

After that I tried subscribing to another investment service. This one takes a different approach. It publishes a newsletter, describing certain stamps that appear to be good items, and then offers to sell them at reasonable rates. Again, I have my doubts. One item offered for sale was a 1973 set of four Australian stamps which they claimed "may be a real 'sleeper.' " The rationale was that this set was printed on two different types of paper and that only a limited number of both types were issued. The newsletter stated that the Stanley Gibbons company offered to sell one variety at $9.60 and that it was asking $144 for the rarer variety. Then it offered to sell sets of both varieties at $4.50 each.

This really baffled me. If Stanley Gibbons was asking $144 for the rarer variety, surely Gibbons would be willing to *buy* the same stamps for, let's say, half that amount. Why on earth would this investment service, which is after all a company that quite legitimately seeks to make a profit, be willing to sell such a set of stamps to its customers for $4.50 if it could sell it to Gibbons for perhaps fifteen times that amount?

Based on such limited information, I don't wish to question the integrity of investment services. But I do question their competence. The types of stamps that they recommend are, in some ways, comparable to certain kinds of oil well stocks. If you strike oil, you will become instantly rich. But the risk is quite high. With the current Wall Street situation, I don't like any of the stocks. But under normal circumstances, I would sleep more soundly if my money were invested not in oil well ventures but in blue chips that have a long history of providing returns to investors.

A sound stamp-investment program will allocate the bulk of its money to blue chips. There is nothing wrong with risking a small amount on recent stamps that appear to be on their way up, but this is like betting on a sixty-to-one shot at the racetrack, and it should be clearly advertised as such. (I'll stick to the three-to-two favorites, thank you.)

Another investment service *does* specialize in the types of stamps that I recommend: nineteenth-century and early-twentieth-century U.S. rarities. But the prices! This company is apparently advertising to non-philatelic prospects, who believe that the *Scott Catalogue* value is the proper price to pay. The company produces a lavish brochure, in glorious full color. It depicts old U.S. stamps and shows their dramatic leap in value over the years. It flashes charts to show that stamps have outpaced Dow Jones Industrials, savings accounts, and mutual funds in the past decade. It offers you a deluxe album in which to store your stamps, which will come to you mounted on a "special display sheet." Then comes the clincher, near the end of the sales letter:

> The price of each investment package will be the current retail value of the stamp or stamps alone, as indicated in the most recent *H.E. Harris Catalog* (for stamps in Average condition) or the *Scott's Specialized Catalogue* (for stamps in Fine condition).

To begin with, a stamp in "Average condition," which may be way off-center, does not constitute a very good investment. As for stamps in Fine condition, they can very often be purchased at well below the *Scott Catalogue* value, as you know.

Take the 1903 James Madison $2 stamp (Scott No. 312), which this company offers to sell you at the 1975 Scott value of $275. The typical auction price for this stamp is $165, and in no case did it sell at auction for above $210. A recent retail ad was offering it for $280 in Extra Fine to Superb condition and $140 in Fine condition.

So this investment company may offer you good material but at rip-off prices. Even if these stamps do appreciate in value at their expected healthy rate, it will take years for you to recover from the high markup that was imposed.

Based on my experience with these three investment services they offered speculative (and, to me, questionable) stamps at good prices or offered good stamps at questionable prices. A true investment broker should offer good stamps at competitive prices. If you can't find one that performs satisfactorily in both areas, I suggest that you buy your own stamps. The auction method is one way to do so.

HOW TO USE AUCTIONS

Millions of dollars worth of rare stamps are sold at auction in the United States each year; perhaps three-fourths of the dollar volume is accounted for by auction galleries in New York City, but there are also major galleries in Philadelphia, Boston, San Francisco, Los Angeles, Detroit, and other large urban centers.

You can deal with all of them by mail. A postcard request will get you the catalogue for the next auction. Sometimes you will be charged a nominal amount (usually 50 cents) for the cost of mailing the catalogue. But once you become a regular bidder, you will be placed on the gallery's mailing list and receive them free. One major gallery in New York estimates that almost 40 percent of the tens of thousands of stamp lots that it sells each year are secured by mailed-in bids.

No matter where you live, you are probably close enough to attend an auction personally. I find them irresistible. If you thrive on competition, you will be back for more. In fact, if you live in the New York City area, you'll find that you can spend a good deal of your spare time at these sales. You will not only enjoy the bidding competition, but you can also meet a fascinating assortment of collectors and dealers.

Late in 1974, I attended an auction held by Robert A. Siegel, Inc., in Manhattan, where about $1 million worth of stamps were sold. That same season, the J&H Stolow Company—a few minutes away by cab or subway—sold $625,000 worth of stamps in a five-day marathon. The Stolow gallery is one of the least attractive auction sites I've seen. It looks like a stock room, with simple folding chairs, long wooden counters, and floor-to-ceiling metal shelving that contains fortunes in stamps unceremoniously packed in cardboard boxes. But Stolow offers a marvelous variety of material and also features "intermissions," when good coffee and delicious pastries are served.

Don't forget, too, that there are major auction galleries in Europe, particularly England and Germany, where certain stamps command far higher or far lower prices than in the United States. Their auction catalogues are sometimes quite lavish, including full-color photographs of choice items.

At this point, you should learn the difference between a "public auction" and a "mail-bid sale." You will see ads for both in the stamp press.

At a public auction, there is competition between those who are present, floor-bidders, and those who have mailed in bids. At a mail-bid sale, *all* bidding is done by mail. I personally prefer the public auction, but I concede that both types have advantages and disadvantages.

HOW TO BUY AT PUBLIC AUCTIONS

Let us suppose that you live in Short Hills, New Jersey, and wish to compete in an auction that will be held three weeks hence in Boston. You send for the catalogue. It arrives in a few days. The first thing to do is read the first page or so *very carefully;* it explains the "Terms of Sale" and comments on the criteria used by this gallery to describe the condition of its stamps. Most galleries use the same jargon, but there are sometimes slight differences that can be critical.

The typical catalogue will have a perforated "bid form," and perhaps an extra copy which you can use as a work sheet. Succeeding pages will list the stamps by "lot number" and offer a brief description of each lot, which can be a single stamp, a set of stamps, or a huge accumulation of stamps that is usually of interest to wholesalers. The description will include the catalogue number of the stamp or stamps described. There will be notes on the condition of the stamp(s), and the current catalogue value will be noted.

By now, you will have in mind that you are in the market for a given list of stamps—those that have a history of steady appreciation in value. You will look for these in the auction catalogue. If you find one in Fine or better condition, make a checkmark next to it.

Now you must decide how much to bid on each item desired. Since there is no guarantee that your bid will be successful, you may see three similar stamps for sale, and want to bid on all of them, with the hope of acquiring just one. You can do so, writing down the lot number and amount bid of each, with the notation "or" in between each lot. Also, you can stay within a budget. If you wish to spend a maximum of $500 at this auction, simply make a prominent note on the bid sheet, saying: "Limit my bids to $500." The moment you have reached this amount, the auctioneer will discard your remaining bids.

Don't forget that when entering a bid you use the lot number, *not* the catalogue number, of the stamps being offered for sale. If you have never dealt with the gallery, jot down references: your bank, membership in philatelic societies, names of other galleries or stamp companies that you've dealt with.

Once you become known to the gallery, they will automatically mail you the stamps that you've acquired, and bill you. If not, they will send you a bill, wait for your check to clear, and then forward the stamps. If you bid by mail, maintain a record of the lot numbers for which you are bidding and the prices you are willing to pay. You can do this on a copy of the bid form or in the margins of the auction catalogue.

When your bid arrives at the gallery, it will be assigned a number, your I.D. for that auction, and listed in the bid book.

HOW AUCTIONEERS OPERATE

The following information is particularly important. When a lot is put up for sale, the opening bid will *not* be the top bid that has been received in the mail. The *second-highest* bid will open up the auction. This works to your advantage, because you can acquire a stamp for a price *lower* than your original bid.

An example. Suppose you have bid $100 for a particular stamp and the next highest mail bid was $85. The auctioneer will open with $85. If there is no competition from the floor bidders, you will get the stamp for the *next advance* above $85. Auctioneers use what is known as a system of "bidding intervals" to advance prices. Here is a common system of bidding intervals:

Bids	Advance	Bids	Advance
Up to $30	$ 1.00	$300–$725	$ 25
$32.50–72.50	$ 2.50	$750–$2,000	$ 50
$75–145	$ 5.00	$2,000–$3,000	$100
$150–290	$10.00	$3,250 and up	$250

In other words, if this is the bidding interval system used at the gallery, a bid within the range of $75 and $145 will be advanced by $5 at a time. Therefore, if the next highest mail bid was $85 and no floor bidders offer higher amounts, you will get the stamp for $90, even though you had bid $100.

Suppose that a floor bidder *does* offer $90, topping the next-highest mail bid. If there is no more bidding, the stamp is yours for $95. In other words, the auctioneer acts as your agent, acquiring the stamps you desire at the lowest possible price. If someone on the floor offers $100, the auctioneer, in your behalf, will respond with, "I already have $100." The floor bidder will have to go to $105 if he wants to top you. If not, the auctioneer will say "$100, to order." The word "order" is a trade term that refers to mail bids.

At this point I should caution you not to make "low-ball" bids, offering ridiculously low prices for good material. The chances are 1 in 1,000 that you will win. You will be merely wasting your time and postage. At a public auction, there is almost always a collector or dealer present who will top you.

HOW MUCH SHOULD YOU BID?

Determining the proper price to bid at auction requires a bit of homework. Take a specific item that I acquired at a Manhattan auction in February 1975.

The item that interested me was a 50-cent slate-blue Columbian of 1893 (Scott No. 240). This stamp catalogued for $35 in 1965 and was up to $120 in 1975. I regard it as a good investment. The catalogue described the stamp as "OG, Fine," meaning that, although it had hinge marks, it retained a good amount of its original gum and was in Fine condition.

The description also said "Photo." Flipping a few pages to the photo section of the auction catalogue, I saw that the stamp was finely centered, and that its perforations appeared to be intact. (When I attended the auction, I arrived several minutes early and asked to inspect the stamp. This is a courtesy extended to all auction bidders, providing you arrive early enough.)

How much to bid? This is when a small reference library comes in handy. Research work should be done in the tranquility of your home, where you can calmly make price comparisons. The pace at a typical auction is too hectic to allow you to do it there. One popular retail price list was asking $140 for this stamp in Fine condition, a full $20 above the *Scott Catalogue* value. But I know from experience that this particular list is subject to discounts.

Another popular retail list (Gibbons), which does not offer discounts, was asking $112. A retail ad in *Linn's Weekly* offered the same stamp, in Fine condition, for $100. All right. I knew I could buy it for sure at $100, providing that retailer was not out of stock.

Next, I looked for the rock bottom value. The H.E. Harris Company, in its *Buying Prices* booklet, was offering $50 to buy this stamp in Good-Fine condition.

A realistic auction bid lay somewhere between the $50 "buy" and the $100 "retail sell" offers.

Next, I looked up this stamp in the 1974 *Green Book of Stamp Auction Prices Realized,* which compiles the results of major galleries around the country. Volume I of *The Green Book* contains information on stamps of the United States and Canada.

The Green Book showed that Scott No. 240 in Fine condition had sold for as low as $40 and as high as $100 the previous year. But the median was $67.50, and this price prevailed on twenty-eight different occasions. Allowing for a possible 15 percent increase in value between 1974 and 1975, I calculated that $77 would be a safe middle-of-the-road bid.

I started at $67.50, but had some competition. I merely kept my hand up, ready to withdraw from the action if the price went beyond $80, my absolute top bid. But when the auctioneer said "$77.50," my hand was the only one still up. The dealers present at the auction had dropped out, because such a bid left them little profit margin for resale. And, lucky for me, there was no die-hard collector in the room willing to spend a high premium for this stamp. I had acquired the stamp at roughly 65 percent of its catalogue value. I will hold it for long-term appreciation. If it continues at its present trend, it will be cataloguing about $250 in five years, and will be salable for about $155. There's no guarantee, of course, but this has been the stamp's trajectory for the past decade.

My methods for arriving at a realistic bid may sound complex upon a first reading. But, with a bit of practice, you can read quickly through a catalogue, check off the items that interest you, and determine a proper bid for each item in a matter of minutes.

MAIL-BIDDING VERSUS FLOOR-BIDDING

As a mail-bidder at a public auction, you have at least one advantage over the floor-bidder. You won't get carried away by the excitement of the auction and bid far more than you intended. I warn you that an auction, particularly when there is spirited bidding for a very desirable stamp, can be almost intoxicating. The floor-bidder does have the advantage of being able to pick up an occasional bargain, when no realistic bids have arrived in the mail.

An example: In October 1974, while attending another auction in New York, I noticed that the catalogue offered a 15-cent green stamp of 1903 (Scott No. 309), which I had routinely checked in the margin as a good item. Between 1965 and 1975 (the 1975 catalogue had just been issued), its value had shot up from $13.50 to $40. The stamp that was being auctioned was described as "OG, Fine" with a "minute gum skip," meaning that a trace of the gum on the back was missing, which is by no means a serious flaw.

Everyone in the gallery must have been dozing. They had

just finished bidding on a series of high-value Columbian stamps, one of which went for $1,100. It was late in the afternoon.

From my reference sources, I knew that the median bid for this stamp last year, in Fine condition, was $24. Harris was offering to buy the stamp, in Fine-Average condition, for $14. Retail lists were selling it for from $22.50 to $45, depending upon condition.

I couldn't believe my ears when the auctioneer opened the bidding with only $7. I routinely raised my hand, and soon found that I had acquired the stamp for $8.50. I wish I could have found one hundred more at the same price. At the very least, I could have sold them to the Harris Company for $14 apiece, making a 76 percent profit overnight.

The next item for sale was the 50-cent orange stamp of the same 1903 set (Scott No. 310). Between 1965 and 1975, the catalogue value of this item had soared from $32.50 to $110. Retail price lists offered it for $82.50. *The Green Book* showed that the year before this stamp in Fine condition like the specimen now being offered had sold for $55 on twenty-four different occasions, and that the lowest price for which it had sold was $38. I recalled that at an auction in Boston the previous week, a similar stamp had gone for $50. I jotted down a note to myself that a good price range for this stamp was $45 to $60.

The opening bid was under $20, and a moment later I acquired it for $22. This is still mystifying to me. I can only surmise that the dealers present at the auction were so mentally exhausted from bidding on the higher-priced items a few moments before that they were indifferent to this modest item. Later that week, a similar stamp sold at an auction elsewhere in the city for $55.

Had it been my stamp, even allowing for the auctioneer's 20 percent commission, I could have doubled my money in just a few days. But that is not the idea. I have put away this stamp for long-term gain, which I'm sure will be quite substantial. Back in

1903, this stamp was first issued in a quantity of 2.6 million copies. Compare this with the fact that current stamps are issued in amounts of 100 million or more, and you'll understand why I'm confident that it will continue to grow in market value.

ARE YOU BIDDING TOO MUCH? OR TOO LITTLE?

You may find, at first, that your auction bids are either too successful, or not successful at all. Either extreme is a warning signal. If you get virtually everything you bid for, you may be offering too much money. If you never win a bid, you are simply not offering competitive prices. With time, you'll develop an instinct for sensible bids. I would suggest that if your batting average is on the low side about one-third of the time, you are probably all right.

In addition to *The Green Book,* remember that the lists of prices realized (available from most galleries a week or two after each auction) are invaluable. Look up the lot numbers of the stamps that you bid for and didn't get. See how much the winning bids paid. Save these lists, together with the auction catalogues. They will guide you in making future bids. There is *no substitute* for hard facts in developing your own bidding instincts.

Some galleries will even offer personal advice in making a competitive bid. Inquire first, and if they are willing, merely send them a list of those lot numbers that interest you. Next to each lot number they will write an estimate of the probable winning bid, and return the list to you (in your own self-addressed envelope). If time is very short, and if you only wish to inquire about a few lots, they might even advise you on the phone. The next step is up to you. Whether you bid or how much you bid is your decision. But the gallery's experience will help assure that your bid is in the ballpark.

HOW TO USE AN AUCTION AGENT

Some collector/investors who cannot personally attend auctions engage the services of an auction agent. One well-known agent, R. Renée Bowden (P. O. Box 348, New York, N. Y. 10023), will search through all New York auction catalogues for specific items that interest you. When she locates these items, she will advise you that they are for sale, and you then advise her by mail of your top bid.

She will personally examine the stamp for you, and execute your bid at the auction. Her fee for searching is 25 cents per country, per catalogue. For executing your bid, she charges 5 percent of the purchase price, with a minimum charge of $5 per auction. Miss Bowden offers to be "your eyes and ears on the New York auction scene."

If you plan to spend important amounts of money, her expertise in checking on a stamp's condition and in gauging a proper price may result in major economies for you. I have never engaged her services, but she is well-known in the trade, and regularly writes a column on auction results for *Linn's Weekly*.

Before leaving the subject of auctions, I urge you to become thoroughly familiar with auction procedures before you start tossing your money around. Several of the major galleries, whose names and addresses are listed on the following pages, offer descriptive literature. Well worth the 25-cent fee is *How to Participate in a Stamp Auction*, a 24-page booklet published by Jacques C. Schiff, Jr., Inc.

A final word: When you bid successfully on a lot of stamps, check them over as soon as they arrive. Make sure the condition is as described. Auction galleries earn a 20 percent commission on the items they sell, without need to engage in dishonest practices. But errors may occur. A stamp may have been graded a notch above its actual condition. And, since the galleries earn more if their items sell for higher prices, it is a human tendency for them to gild the lily a bit.

If you discover any discrepancy, return the stamp immediately by resigtered mail, with a letter demanding a refund. If in doubt as to a stamp's condition or authenticity, contact the gallery and request an extension of time, so that you can have the stamp "expertized." No reputable gallery will refuse to cooperate, providing you have reasonable grounds for your doubts.

You can avoid much of this trouble if you read the auction catalogue description of each stamp with some care. If a stamp is described as being in Average or Very Good condition, don't expect it to have Fine centering. If the catalogue says that the stamp is missing a perforation tooth or has a thin, it is assumed that you were aware of this when you entered your bid. In short, read carefully beforehand, and it is unlikely that you will be involved in disputes later.

SOME U.S. AUCTION GALLERIES

Here is a list of some galleries that regularly conduct auctions of postage stamps. This is by no means an all-inclusive list. But it tells you where to write, visit, or call for catalogues of near-future auctions. Ads in *Linn's Weekly* and other stamp publications will advise you of future auctions. This list also gives you an idea of the various geographic locations of major auction galleries:

- Advanced Philatelics, 5410 Wilshire Blvd., Suite 208, Los Angeles, California 90036.
- Earl P.L. Apfelbaum, Inc. 1420 Walnut St., Philadelphia, Pa. 19102. Tel. (215) 985-1550.
- Hugh C. Barr, 38 Park Row, New York, N.Y. 10038.
- Fritz Billig, 168-39 Highland Ave., Jamaica, N.Y. 11432.

(Regularly holds auctions at the Commodore Hotel in New York City.)

- Ted Conway, P.O. Box 420, Lynbrook, N.Y. 11563. (Holds monthly auctions of U.S. stamps.)
- Cherrystone Stamp Center, 132 West 34th St., New York, N.Y. 10001. Tel. (212) 947-3256.
- Eastland Stamp Auctions, Concourse, Eastland Center, Harper Woods, Mich. 48225. Tel. (313) 371-8864.
- William A. Fox, 263 White Oak Ridge Rd., Short Hills, N.J. 07078.
- David F. Gilbert, Inc., 1744 E. 17th St., Brooklyn, N.Y. 11229. Tel. (212) 336-8312.
- H.R. Harmer, Inc. 6 West 48th St., New York, N.Y. 10036. Tel. (212) 757-4460.
- Harmer, Rooke & Co., Inc. 3 East 57th St., New York, N.Y. 10022. Tel. (212) 751-1900.
- Irvin Heiman, Inc. 21243 Ventura Blvd., Suite 104. Woodland Hills, Cal. 91364.
- Great Lakes Stamp Auctions, 6687 Northwest Highway, Chicago, Ill. 60631. Tel. (312) 763-6693.
- John W. Kaufmann, Inc., 1010 Vermont Ave., N.W., Washington, D.C. 20005. Tel. (202) 638-5658.
- Daniel Kelleher Co., Inc. 40 Court St., Boston, Mass. 02108.
- Peter Kenedi of California, Inc. 15300 Ventura Blvd., Suite 304, Sherman Oaks, Cal. 91403. Tel. (213) 986-5990.
- Kenton Stamp Auctions. Box 8472, Kansas City, Mo. 64114.
- Robert E. Lippert, 16953 E. Warren Ave., Detroit, Mich. 48224.
- Greg Manning Co., Inc. 76 South Orange Ave., South Orange, N.J. 07079. Tel. (201) 762-7660.
- Vahan Mozian, Inc. 147 W. 42nd St., New York, N.Y. 10036.

- Paramount Philatelics. Paramount Bldg., Englewood, Ohio, 45322. Tel. (513) 836-3766.
- Philatelic Center, Inc. 692 Lexington Ave., New York, N.Y. 10022. Tel. (212) 753-0225.
- Jacques C. Schiff, Jr., Inc. 536 West 111th St., New York, N.Y. 10025. Tel. (212) 662-2777.
- Robert A. Siegel, Inc. 120 East 56th St., New York, N.Y. 10022. Tel. (212) 753-6421.
- Simmy's Stamp Co., Inc. 40 Court St., Boston, Mass. 02108.
- J.&H. Stolow, Inc. 915 Broadway, New York, N.Y. 10010. Tel. (212) 533-0790.
- Superior Stamp & Coin Co., 517 West 7th St., Los Angeles, Cal. 90004.
- Wilshire Stamp Co., 411 N. Larchmont Blvd., Los Angeles, Cal. 90004.
- Jackson Winter, Inc., 11941 Wilshire Blvd., Los Angeles, Cal. 90025 .
- Richard Wolffers, Inc., 127 Kearny St., San Francisco, Cal. 94108. Tel. (415) 781-5127.

SOME AUCTION GALLERIES ABROAD

Here are a few major auction galleries outside of the United States.

- Arnold Ebel. Zeil 79, Frankfurt M6, Germany. [This gallery has produced 500-page catalogues, with as many as 150 full-color photos. The U.S. representative is John G. Ross, 12 West Madison St., Chicago, Ill. 60602. His phone number is (312) 236-4088.]
- Stanley Gibbons, Ltd. 391 Strand, London, WC2R OLX, England.

- Bournemouth Stamp Auctions, The Auction House, 39 Poole Hill, Bournemouth BH2 5PX, England.
- Robson Lowe, Ltd., 50 Pall Mall, London SW1 Y 5JZ, England.
- Vance Auctions. PO Box 195, Stoney Creek, Ontario, Canada L8G 3X9. Tel. (416) 561-2125.
- Warwick & Warwick. 35-37 Albert St. Rugby, Warwickshire, England.

MAIL-BID SALES AND AUCTIONS

A sale of stamps where *all* bids are received in the mail (there are no floor bidders) has some inherent dangers.

To begin with, such a sale does not require a licensed auctioneer. The entire sale may be conducted upon the kitchen table of a part-time stamp dealer, whose honesty and reputation are difficult to discern at a distance.

Secondly, you cannot bid high, with confidence that should you win your bid will be reduced to the "normal advance" above the next-highest bid. You must depend totally upon the integrity of the person conducting this private auction.

For this reason, I much prefer public auctions. Even though I can't personally attend all of them, I have some reasonable assurance that other floor-bidders present are keeping the proceedings honest.

This is not a blanket indictment of all mail sales. Some mail-sale firms have been in business for years, and I assume have provided satisfactory service to buyers. A few of them will even offer a list of prices realized.

The advantage of mail sales is that they frequently offer for sale small medium-priced lots of material that larger auction galleries do not bother with.

Try one, if you wish. But I suggest that you bid lower than

you would if it were a public auction. This protects you from the possibility that the "auctioneer" will not reduce your winning bid to one interval above the next highest offer.

You will find numerous mail sales advertised in the stamp press.

USEFUL PRICE LISTS

Some stamp companies have a faithful clientele of collector/investors that purchase regularly from their price lists. A few of these companies offer "one of a kind" collections that they have purchased, frequently at large discounts. There is no guarantee that your check will be the first to arrive, but it will be promptly refunded if someone else beats you to it. Other items are available in large quantities, and offer a fairly good guarantee that you will get the merchandise.

The stamp press features ads for many companies that offer such lists. If you wish to inquire immediately, here are a few of the frequent advertisers:

- Richard H. Dresel. PO Box 628, West Englewood Station, Teaneck, N.J. 07666. $5 gets you a first-class-mail 20-month subscription to his list of ten to twelve pages, which offers intact collections, stamps on album pages, single stamps, sets, and rarities.
- Bombay Philatelic Company. 65 Nassau St. New York, N.Y. 10038. A six-by-nine-inch stamped, self-addressed envelope will get you their twelve-page list of "in-depth" stock, which specializes in British Commonwealth.
- Kanmar Stamp Company. 27 Florence Drive. Syosett, N.Y. 11791. Mails out a list of better stamps to its Select Inner Circle Club.
- Monthly Scholl Bulletin. PO Box 123, Batavia, Ohio

45103. In business since 1936. Mails out a monthly bulletin which costs $2 per year.

- Flushing Philatelics. PO Box 951, Linden Hill Station, Flushing, N.Y. 11354. Charges $2 for ten bi-monthly issues of its wholesale price list.

- Eddicks. PO Box 103. Fairfield, California 94533. This monthly list costs $3 per year and offers collections, lots, singles.

- R.G. Provost Co. PO Box 398. Schenectady, N.Y. 12301. Its monthly bulletin, *The Bargain Counter,* costs $5 per year, but is mailed free to those who buy $75 or more per year worth of stamps.

- Summit Stamps. 5410 Wilshire Blvd. Suite No. 408. Los Angeles, California 90036. Has a wholesale list, with minimum orders at $20.

- Herman Most. 11900 Devilwood Dr., Rockville, Md. 20854. His mailing list costs $3 per year and offers mainly nineteenth-century collections.

- Edward Berman. Box 44. Plainview, N.Y. 11803. Offers stamps on old album pages, at large discounts, from 50 to 75 percent off *Scott Catalogue* value.

Another word of caution. The fact that a dealer offers stamps at "wholesale prices" could mean nothing. It is possible that you may find a retail ad in *Linn's Weekly* or *Stamps* magazine, for example, at equal or lower prices. The selling price of a stamp is based upon what it cost the seller to acquire that stamp. If he made a good purchase from a collector and is not too greedy, he may, indeed, offer you a bargain. But not necessarily. Before buying from a wholesale price list, double-check some of the current retail ads and compare. As a rule, you will find that wholesale lists do offer lower prices. But there are frequent exceptions. Some large retailers may also occasionally acquire stamps at rock-bottom prices and be willing to pass along the savings to you, with attractive discounts.

If you take time to compare prices, you can find real bargains. This is why I suggested at the outset of this chapter that you develop a variety of sources.

CHAPTER 8

HOW TO GUARD AGAINST FORGERIES AND FAKES

As in all fields of collecting—coins, antiques, fine art, for example—there is always some chance that you have paid for something which is falsely represented.

The vast majority of postage stamps are genuine, but it would be naive to pretend that there is absolutely no risk of their being forgeries or fakes. To begin with, you should know the difference between these two terms as they are employed in the philatelic world.

A forgery is a fraudulent imitation of a genuine stamp.

A fake is a genuine stamp that has been "improved" in some way, to enhance its value. Its back may have been regummed to change its status from unused to mint; if it was used, its cancellations may have been skillfully erased, to make it appear unused; a missing perforation tooth may have been added;

155

it may have been altered in some way, thus changing a common stamp to a rare variety.

Some forgeries are so masterful that they have evoked widespread admiration, and have even created a following of collectors.

THE GREATEST FORGER OF THEM ALL

Perhaps the world's most famous (or should we say notorious?) stamp forger was the late Jean de Sperati, an Italian expert in paper and chemicals who resided in France until his death in 1957 at the age of seventy-three. During his long career, the ingenious Sperati forged hundreds of rare and semi-rare stamps from dozens of countries, including eighty-nine issues from his native France and five different U.S. stamps. In a few cases, this brilliant forger even acquired remnants of the paper used to print authentic stamps, making it even more difficult to detect his forgeries.

When the Paris courts caught up with him in 1952, Sperati defiantly published a book-length apologia, called *Against the Experts*. He was proudest, he said, of his die proofs, each of which he signed below the design, for posterity. In 1954, the admiring British Philatelic Association even published a book that listed and illustrated many of Sperati's forgeries; the limited edition of 500 copies of this book sold for 24 pounds per volume.

In 1974, at an auction in London's Stanley Gibbons gallery, a Sperati forgery of a 1913 Australian stamp realized a higher price than was normally bid on the genuine article. Said the Gibbons auction catalogue: "Sperati considered himself a master artist, and did not regard his productions as forgeries, but rather as works of art. He fabricated them with extreme care and spared no effort to improve them as he found necessary."

More recently, there was the case of Raoul de Thuin, a

Belgian who resided in Yucatan, Mexico, for four decades and produced numerous forgeries of stamps from thirty-one countries. Finally, officials of the American Philatelic Society made a pilgrimage to Yucatan and after several days of negotiation acquired all of his equipment and stock, as well as his signed agreement to terminate his activities. The latest word is that the elderly de Thuin now lives in Guayaquil, Ecuador, where he paints and sells pictures, and—for a fee—will recount his forgery exploits to visiting philatelists.

More frequently than not, forged U.S. stamps have been of common varieties, produced en masse to avoid postal costs, and not to defraud collectors. Such is the case of a recent 8-cent Eisenhower stamp that has turned up. One of the few high-priced U.S. stamps known to be forged is the $2.60 Graf Zeppelin issue of 1930 (Scott No. C15). These were believed to have originated in Paris in the early 1950s, when genuine copies were retailing for about $55. Today, the catalogue price for this stamp is $525. However, the forgery is quite crude when compared side-by-side with an original.

While this is all interesting, it is of little consolation if you buy an apparently genuine stamp and find it to be a forgery or a fake. Just what *are* the chances for this occurring?

HOW GREAT IS YOUR RISK?

Let's take a look at the five high values of the 1893 Columbian issue (Scott Nos. 241–245), which appear to be tempting targets for forgers and fakers. According to the experience of the Philatelic Foundation in Manhattan, only 23 of the 567 high-value Columbians submitted to it for scrutiny were forgeries; this is a mere 4 percent.

The greatest hazard lies in the area of fakes. Of the 567 high-value Columbians examined by the Philatelic Foundation,

113 (about 20 percent) had been regummed. This means that if you pay a substantial premium for never-hinged Columbians, the chances are one in five that you are paying too much. The stamp may have had no gum at all, or there may have been hinge marks on the original gum, but the faker adroitly "improved" this stamp to "mint" condition, giving it a pristine gum surface on the back. Another 36 stamps of the 567 Columbians (about 6 percent) were genuine, but had been reperforated, also vastly increasing their market value.

In 1974, for example, the *Scott Catalogue* value of a $4 Columbian (Scott No. 244) was $725. At auctions that year, Very Fine copies sold for a median of $675. But Very Fine copies that were never-hinged sold at auction for prices of $900, $1,000, even $1,350. This is a very high premium to pay for a minuscule amount of gum, particularly if it was added to the stamp by a faker.

Even among the lower values of the Columbian series, gum was a major price factor. At auction, the 30-cent stamp of that series (Scott No. 239) in Very Fine condition sold for a median of $75. If it was never-hinged, the median price jumped to $115.

Which is why I again advise you *not* to become a "never-hinged fetishist," as many modern collectors are; the extra value of this gum, even when originally applied by the postal authorities, is dubious; and to pay extra for the works of a faker adds insult to injury.

WATCH OUT FOR "REISSUES"

Another series to watch out for are the 1875 Reissues (Scott Nos. 123-132), almost all of which qualify as excellent investments. These stamps are reissues, with slight differences, of the 1869 first pictorial series of the United States (Scott Nos. 112-122). In most cases, the reissues of 1875 have higher market values.

Of the 1,114 so-called reissues submitted to the Philatelic Foundation, it was found that *only 637* (about 57 percent) were absolutely genuine. Only 100 (8 percent) were not genuine, or forgeries. Small percentages were also either regummed, or reperforated. But the real danger lay in the 253 stamps (22 percent) that were merely genuine, and cheaper, stamps from the original 1869 pictorial series that were being passed off as 1875 reissues. For example, the 30-cent blue and carmine stamp of the 1869 series (Scott No. 121) has a current catalogue value of $500. The look-alike 30-cent reissue of 1875 is valued at $775.

COIL STAMPS ARE SUPER-RISKY

Coil stamps are a great potential area for fakers and forgers. Starting in 1908, the post office began to issue stamps in coils for use in vending machines. Coil stamps, as you know, are issued with perforations on two sides only, either top and bottom or left and right. One relatively simple way to create a coil stamp from a common stamp that is perforated on all sides (providing that it has wide margins around the design) is to clip away the perforations at top and bottom, or at the two sides. Another way is to add perforations to two sides of an imperforate stamp.

The first coil stamp was the 1-cent blue-green portrait of Benjamin Franklin (Scott No. 316), a pair of which is valued at $8,500. There is a similar-looking stamp issued in 1906 (Scott No. 314), which was produced imperforate and is worth $17.50. Many of these have had perforations added at top and bottom, to resemble the extremely scarce coil stamp. In fact, of 109 specimens of the No. 316 coil submitted to the Philatelic Foundation, *83 percent were not genuine.*

Between 1908 and 1922, about twenty-five different coil stamps were issued, and many of these are quite rare. Such coils must be approached with extreme caution. Another example is the 2-cent carmine coil stamp of 1910 (Scott No. 388), which catalogues for $90. There is a nearly-identical 2-cent carmine stamp of 1911 (Scott No. 384) which was issued imperforate and now catalogues for only $2.75. If the latter stamp has wide margins, it is no great task to create perforations at both sides and illegally upgrade this stamp to thirty times its true value.

This does not mean that you should refrain completely from purchasing coil stamps that have investment potential. But you must be careful. In some cases, purchasing a coil pair lessens the risk of it being a fake.

You'll find another look-alike problem with the bluish-paper issue of 1909 (Scott Nos. 357–366), that resemble more common stamps of that period, but are quite rare. An analysis of 1,218 bluish-paper stamps submitted to the Philatelic Foundation found that only 63 percent were genuine.

To simplify matters, particularly at the beginning, when you are less knowledgeable, you might restrict your investments to those stamps that have no genuine look-alikes. Famous commemorative sets such as the Columbians of 1893 and the Trans-Mississippis of 1898 are issued in only one format. There can be no cases of mistaken identity. You will find many of these, so there will be no lack of stamps in which to invest. A perusal of the *Scott Catalogue* will enable you to single them out.

HOW TO USE EXPERTIZING SERVICES

For a small fee roughly equivalent to an insurance premium, you can determine whether your stamp acquisitions are genuine. Both the American Philatelic Society and the Philatelic Foundation offer what is known as an "expertizing service"; they will examine your stamps and render an opinion on their authenticity. Not only will your mind be set at ease, but the value of your stamps will be enhanced when you wish to sell, because collectors have confidence in a stamp when it is accompanied by an APS or PF certificate.

The APS charges $4 to expertize a stamp that catalogues for $200 or less, $6 for items in the $200 to $1,000 value range, and $9 for those worth $1,000 or more. To avail yourself of this service, you must write to the American Philatelic Expertization Service, Box 800, State College, Pa. 16801.

The Philatelic Foundation, 99 Park Ave., New York, N.Y. 10016 charges $10 to examine a stamp valued at $500 or more. For any item above $500, the cost is 2 percent of catalogue value, up to a maximum charge of $500. You are charged the minimum ($10) if your stamp is judged not to be genuine. The Philatelic Foundation issues a blue-green certificate for genuine stamps, and a buff-colored certificate for those judged to be "other than genuine": reperforated, regummed, cleaned, faked, or outright counterfeits. A photograph of the stamp is affixed to the certificate and sealed with the PF seal.

THE OVERALL RISKS ARE NOT GREAT

In summary, stamp fakes and forgeries do not constitute a major menace to the collector/investor. They are far more common in certain types of stamps, such as coils and look-alike issues where one variety is far more valuable than its near twin. The most frequent offense is the "improvement" of genuine stamps, particularly by applying new gum to the back.

As in all affairs relating to money, common sense and a reasonable degree of caution help considerably. Above all, if you purchase an expensive stamp, keep a record of where and when you bought it. If the stamp is not genuine, you can make a claim for refund. It is doubtful that a reputable dealer or auctioneer would jeopardize his good name and future business, providing you have adequate proof of purchase.

If you carefully read the "Conditions of Sale" of auction catalogues that you receive, you will see that reputable galleries offer you a fair opportunity. The conditions outlined in a recent sale by Greg Manning Auctions, Inc., are illustrative of what I mean. When in the "opinion of any competent authority" the stamps you purchased are not genuine, "the purchase price will be refunded in full."

You should be aware of time limits, however. Most galleries allow you four weeks, which is quite reasonable. If, for any reason, it takes more than four weeks to receive an expert opinion, you can get an extension, providing you request one in writing. The Manning Company also offers to pay the cost of expertizing the stamp, up to a maximum of $50. In the case of U.S. stamps, Manning and most other galleries recognize the Philatelic Foundation as an acceptable expertizing body.

A final thought on this subject: Don't be wholly dependent upon expert help in identifying fakes or forgeries. A *Scott Catalogue,* a color guide, a perforation gauge, a magnifying glass, and a bit of patience are all that's needed to spot the more obvious attempts at deception. Scrutinize every important stamp acquisition that you make. Slowly, you will come to recognize the features of certain stamps. If you purchase multiples of a particular item, examine them all carefully under a magnifying glass. Compare them. Pay particular attention to details of the design, to the perforation gauge, to shades of color. Such scrutiny will help you to avoid being defrauded, and make you a far more knowledgeable collector/investor.

Virtually all dealers and auctioneers will refund your money if stamps that they sold you (even if genuine) are not "as described." That is, if a stamp is said to be Very Fine, yet its design is obviously far off-center, even a cursory look will determine that the description was overly optimistic. Or if a stamp is described as Fine but is missing a perforation tooth, or has a tiny tear, a magnifying glass will quickly reveal these flaws. With a bit of practice, you can become fairly expert, and don't hesitate to request a refund. Don't be a pest, however. The auctioneer is being forthright in admitting that a stamp has a flaw when the catalogue description says: "Very Fine appearance, tiny thin." Don't focus on the former and neglect the latter. Read auction catalogues carefully *before* you bid.

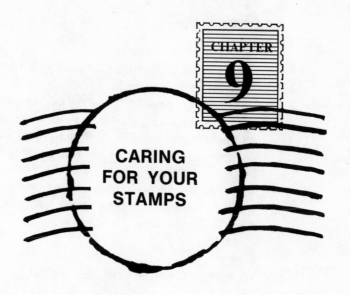

CHAPTER 9

CARING FOR YOUR STAMPS

Stamps are reasonably easy to care for. But they are, after all, pieces of paper. Pound for pound—ounce for ounce, I should say—they might be your most valuable possessions. Their value can be decimated by a crease, tear or smudge, or by excessive heat or humidity; they can also be stolen.

First of all, you should give some thought to what method of stamp storage you will use. You will simplify matters tremendously if you store all of your acquisitions in a bank safety deposit box.

But life is usually more complex. I have yet to meet the stamp collector who doesn't enjoy immediate access to his holdings. When a friend comes for dinner, and when the cordials and cigars are served, it can be an almost irresistible temptation to show off your collection. Or, you may wish to pore over it in the evenings, as a form of relaxation.

If you install a strong safe at home this problem is resolved. Your stamps will always be within easy reach. But you may not wish to incur the expense or bother of such an installation. If this is the case, you might consider the following compromise. Keep an album or two of stamps at home, to satisfy your natural urge to inspect them. But if you purchase multiple copies of a particular stamp or an especially valuable item, keep these in a bank safety deposit box. By dividing your holdings in this way, with the bulk of your investment protected by the bank, you avoid total loss from fire, flood, or theft and at the same time can enjoy your collection on a day-to-day basis.

HOW TO KEEP YOUR STAMP RECORDS

No matter what system you devise, record-keeping is essential. By keeping proper records you will know at a glance the value of your holdings. In case of loss you will know the value of that loss. When you wish to sell all or part of your collection, you will have an accurate picture of your profits.

Here is a simple method of record-keeping. Purchase a stack of three-by-five-inch index cards and a small box to hold them. Each card will represent a stamp or set of stamps, and be kept by country in numerical order, according to *Scott Catalogue* number. After a year or so, here is what a typical card might look like:

U.S. 240 *

6-18-75	F-VF	$120	Harmer	(album)
8-30-75	F, OG	$90	Stolow	
2-15-76	VF	$160	Siegel	

By now, you can probably guess the meaning of the card's content. In the upper corner, we have identified the 50-cent slate-blue stamp of the 1893 Columbian Issue (Scott No. 240), with the asterisk meaning that it is unused. On June 18, 1975, you purchased a Fine-Very Fine copy of the stamp for $120 at the Harmer auction. You placed that stamp in the album which you keep at home. On August 30, you purchased a Fine copy (with original gum) of the same stamp for $90 at the Stolow auction. It is being kept in your bank safety deposit box. On February 15 of the next year, you purchased a Very Fine copy for $160 at the Siegel gallery. It too, is in the bank.

I think you'll agree that this is a simple method, requiring only a moment's time when you acquire each stamp. This little file can be kept at home to provide a complete record of your holdings. Only in the very unlikely event that a fire completely destroyed your home would such a record be obliterated. But even then all is not lost. You see, when you purchase a stamp at auction, or by any other method, there is always an invoice, showing the source of purchase, the stamp's catalogue number, its condition, and its price. These invoices can be kept together with the stamps in the safety deposit box. For those better stamps that you keep at home in an album, store the invoices at the bank, adding the note "album" on them.

HOW TO HANDLE STORAGE PROBLEMS

If you follow my advice, you will collect the stamps of one or two countries at most. Purchase a specialized album of each. Scott, Harris, White Ace, Minkus and Lighthouse all manufacture top quality albums. Most of them also sell cheaper albums for neophyte collectors. Buy the best available and you won't regret it. The Scott U.S. National Album costs about $25 and is well worth it, providing spaces for every conceivable variety of stamp, and offering maximum protection with its high grade paper and sturdy covers.

Store your albums vertically, as you would a book. If you let them rest horizontally, pages will be pressed tightly together, and stamps with gum may (especially during periods of high humidity) become stuck to the pages, causing irreparable damage. If you store your stamps in glassine or acetate envelopes, the same principle holds true; store them vertically, and don't pack them tightly together.

Talking about envelopes, the most popular variety is the glassine, which has a milky transparency, and is available almost everywhere. If you prefer absolute transparency, as many auction houses do when they display their stamps, check out the clear mylar envelopes offered by John M. Blood, Jr., 380 High St., Holyoke, Mass. 01040, which cost only a few dollars per box of 500.

As I mentioned before, extreme humidity can be a problem with unused stamps, mainly because of the gum on the back. I wouldn't air condition my house just for the sake of my stamps, but I *would* store them in a room that is already air-conditioned. If humidity is a serious problem in your home, write to Collectors National Stamp Service, 139 Rockway Ave., Suite Six, Weymouth, Mass. 02188. They sell a substance called Sorb-it which can be stored with your stamps, to pick up excessive moisture.

Light is not too serious a menace, but excessive amounts of sunlight or fluorescent lighting can fade the colors on stamps. Simply keep your albums in a dark place when you're not viewing them.

Collectors National Stamp Service also sells for $15 a fascinating *Dealer's Guide to Chemical Restoration of Postage Stamps.* It all depends upon how deeply you wish to delve into philately, but you can learn a great deal from this treatise.

If you do decide to install a safe in your house, scan your local classified section for notices of used safes for sale. The stamp press also occasionally features ads of new safes for collectors. Recently, the J. Goodman Company, Box 88, Livingston, N.J. 07039, and the Nor-Gee Corporation, Box 6L, Lancaster N.Y. 14086, have offered modestly priced home safes in these ads. I can't vouch for their quality, but you might send for a catalogue to check specifications for strength and fire resistance.

HOW TO REDUCE THE RISK OF THEFT

The odds are against it, but you must face the possibility that the stamps you keep at home may be stolen.

If you go away on vacation, you will sleep more soundly in your beach-front cabana if your stamps are not lying around at home. Leave them with a friend or relative. Or check with your bank. Banks sometimes accept packages for bulk storage on a temporary basis. If so, you might put your album or albums in a sturdy container, such as a whiskey bottle case, seal it and leave it with the bank.

As a member of the American Philatelic Society, you have some added protection. If stamps are stolen, report this loss to Mrs. Maryette B. Lane, 490 23rd Ave. North, St. Petersburg, Fla. 33704, Tel. (813) 898-7238. Providing you have a good description of the missing stamps, the APS will spread the word. In numerous cases, stolen stamps have been recovered.

Also, the APS offers low-cost, all-risk stamp insurance to its members. A special feature is an automatic 1 percent increase in the amount of insurance every second month (to take care of new acquisitions and/or increases in value). Coverage is written for one-year terms, continued automatically, and a reduction in premium is allowed if you store the stamps in a bank vault or safe. Details of this plan are available from the APS Insurance Plan, Box 5789, Baltimore, Md., 21208.

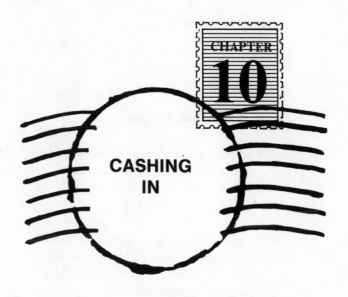

CHAPTER 10

CASHING IN

The day will inevitably arrive when you wish to cash in all or some of your stamp properties.

Before you do, examine your motives. If you have simply lost interest, and wish to invest your assets in something else, that is certainly your prerogative.

However, if you have not retained your stamps for at least a few years, you might ask yourself why you purchased them in the first place. If you sell too soon, you will barely recoup your investment. And if you feel that you must sell because of some unexpected cash need, it is very possible that you were overinvesting in the first place. Investment should make use of spare assets, not those which are momentary surplus and might be needed for some emergency. So before you spend a penny on stamps, be reasonably certain that you are prepared for long-term investment. That is the only way to achieve the profits that you seek.

AN ALTERNATIVE TO SELLING

Whatever the reason, let us suppose that you do require cash, and your stamps represent your least essential assets. Selling is not the only solution. Don't panic and divest yourself of precious assets that have taken time and money to accumulate.

Perhaps the best proof of the intrinsic value of rare stamps is the fact that you can use them as collateral for loans, without credit investigations, and in absolute privacy.

If you don't want to sell, consider a loan. Several organizations specialize in loans to owners of stamps, rare coins, and gems.

The Provident Loan Society of New York, 346 Park Avenue South, New York, N.Y. 10010, Tel. (212) 685-0380, is one such organization. For recent U.S. mint stamps (sheets, blocks and plate blocks) they will lend you an amount up to 65 percent of the face value of your property. For rare stamps that have reached premium status, loans are based on auction sale values. They will also accept mint album collections of U.S. singles, providing sets are complete and contain some of the early singles and souvenir sheets. This organization does not accept UN or foreign stamps as collateral.

Provident will make a loan appraisal of your stamp holdings free of charge. Loans are made for one year, with interest charged at 15 percent per annum. If your stamps are appreciating at this rate, you are more or less breaking even on the interest, while making use of their loan monies.

One attractive feature about such loans is that there are no lengthy forms to fill out, or complicated credit checks to go through. The value of your collection speaks for itself. In a matter of a few hours (or a couple of days if you deal by mail) you can have the needed cash in hand.

Other companies that provide loans for philatelic holdings are:

- Fidelity Capital Company, 1869 Broadway, N.Y. 10023. Tel. (212) 757-5185. Loans range from $50 to $15,000 for a single stamp, and from $50 to $100,000 for a collection.
- S.H. Engel & Co., Inc., 38 Park Row, New York, N.Y. 10038. Offers loans on U.S. and foreign stamps.
- Edelman's, 301 Old York Road, Jenkintown, Pa. 19046. This company offers "quick, confidential loans" of "up to 80 percent of the value" of the properties, and allows 30 months to pay.

By using the loan route, you retain ownership of your collection and its value continues to build, while the loan company keeps the stamps in its vaults. When your financial status improves, you can repay the loan and get your stamps back. In the worst of cases, if you cannot pay off the loan, the stamps will be put up for public auction. If the stamps realize a price higher than the amount you owe, you get the difference.

SO YOU WANT TO SELL

You have decided to sell all or part of your stamp investment portfolio. The best advice that I can give is to offer you an adaptation of the old saying: "He that sells in haste shall repent at leisure."

There are countless horror stories of collectors or their heirs trying to sell stamps who have put themselves at the mercy of unscrupulous buyers. A shrewd buyer can spot the novice and will think of numerous ways to downgrade the value of the seller's stamps.

Not long ago, a stamp dealer from Boulder, Colorado, complained that even he was nearly taken by some of his colleagues. A distant relative of his had died. Since the dealer specialized only in stamps of the British Pacific, and the collection of the deceased consisted largely of the United States, Great Britain, and Canada, the dealer decided to sell the collection rather than buy it for himself. He examined it, found it was 99 percent mint in Very Fine condition, and its *Scott Catalogue* value was $38,050. He calculated that it should command at least $30,000 at retail.

The dealer was planning to take a trip across the United States, so he decided to call upon some of the largest stamp firms in the country.

One company on the East Coast offered him $5,000 and had the audacity to tell him that his stamps would be worth more if they were postally used. Another company offered him $7,200, claiming that some of the early British and Canadian stamps were forgeries.

A third dealer said that he would pay "100 percent of catalogue value" and then produced a catalogue of very mysterious origin. Tapping away at his adding machine, he totaled up the figures and offered $8,756.78. This was the highest offer that the Colorado dealer received on the East Coast.

On the West Coast, he met one man who claimed to have an immediate buyer and offered $7,500. Furthermore, he offered to reduce his usual commission from 20 percent to 10 percent, and said he could provide a check "right now" for $6,750. He was refused. The dealer became upset, and the Colorado man then revealed his own status as a dealer. Whereupon the prospective buyer suddenly increased his offer to $12,000. The Colorado man walked out, his faith in mankind substantially deflated.

This could happen to you if you're not careful.

HOW TO FIGURE OUT YOUR BEST PRICE

The most important step in selling is to know the value of what you have. This is why I emphasize that you should keep careful records as you acquire each stamp, noting down its condition and cost, as well as its present catalogue value.

When you plan to sell, sit down and make a detailed list of your holdings, item by item, listed in numerical order by catalogue number. You should note the condition of each stamp and its catalogue value at present. By totaling this up, you have a rough idea of the top figure attainable for these stamps.

Then, consult some reliable source such as the buying list of the Harris Company, which will provide you with a bottom figure. Do a little more checking around on your better properties. Consult *The Green Book* of auction prices realized and see what both dealers and collectors are currently paying for these stamps in free competition. Check over the "buy" ads in the stamp press, to see whether certain dealers might be especially eager for some of your better material. Jot down the prices. This will be immensely helpful in insuring that an unscrupulous dealer won't take advantage of you.

Let's see how such a listing would work for one stamp:

$3 1898 COLUMBIAN (#243), FINE, LH

1965 Cat. Value	My Cost	1975 Cat. Value	1975 Harris "Buy"	1974 Auction Avg.	1975 Linn's "Buy" Ad
$140.	$90.	$625.	$250.	$320.	$300.

Now you have an idea of the worth of your stamp. In 1965, when it catalogued for $140, you purchased it at auction for $90. This has been a real winner. In ten years, its catalogue value has soared to $625. It's hard to find at retail for under $400. The Harris Company offers to buy it from you for $250. This is your rock-bottom price. A dealer advertising in *Linn's* offers $300. At auction the previous year, this stamp sold for as low as $230, as high as $500, but most frequently (20 times) at $320.

If you sell it at auction for $320, you will pay about 20 percent commission to the gallery, reducing your net proceeds to $256. On the other hand, the stamp has appreciated nearly 25 percent in value since last year. It might auction for $400 or more. If it brings in $400, your share, after the gallery commission, would be $320. This is a $230 profit over your original cost, a net gain of 255 percent, meaning that it grew in value by better than 12 percent per year.

You can take your chances at auction, or offer the stamp to the fellow advertising in *Linn's* at $300, not a bad profit either ($210, also representing average yearly gain of better than 12 percent).

No matter what mode of sale you try, you now have at least some idea of the worth of this stamp. The worst situation imaginable is to approach a dealer with a stamp for sale, and not be ready with a reply when he asks "How much do you want?" Even the most honest dealer will be tempted to offer a ridiculously low amount if you appear to be so ill-prepared.

If you have collected over a number of years, your stamps can be worth thousands of dollars. It is worth your time to spend a few evenings at home, compiling a list of your properties, and setting their minimum value.

HERE'S HOW TO GO ABOUT IT

Once you have done this, you can explore various methods of selling. You can ask a dealer to make you an offer. If the collection is large enough, he will visit your home. For a fee, he will appraise the value of your collection, and usually waive the fee if you sell the stamps to him.

You can mail your stamps (registered, of course) to one of the many dealers who regularly advertise in the philatelic press for collections, or for material from specific countries. The normal practice of many of these dealers is to mail you a check, which constitutes their offer for the properties you have mailed them. If the check is for a ridiculously low amount, simply return it and ask for the return of your stamps. In other cases, the offer may be close to your asking price, and you may be able to negotiate it upward. If the offer is satisfactory, simply cash the check and send him a note. The deal is concluded.

You may, instead, prefer to reply to "buy" ads that offer specific prices for individual stamps or sets. These prices are sometimes quite generous, and by selling your stamps individually in this manner, you may well profit by this method. The only trouble is that once you have sold the stamps requested in the "buy" ads you are stuck with the remainder of your collection, which sometimes consists of less desirable material (less desirable in the sense that dealers are not so anxious to buy it because they have adequate inventories). This leftover material will have to be disposed of at a considerable discount.

One experienced dealer recently wrote: "There is often as much larceny in the heart of the seller as there is in the buyer. . . . There is no substitute for knowledge and fair play on the part of both the buyer and the seller."

In order to realize the best possible price for your stamps, keep in mind the structure of the philatelic market.

If you sell to a stamp wholesaler, a "dealers' dealer," you must appreciate his dilemma. He has to acquire your stamps at a low enough price to tack on his own commission when he sells to a retailer, who in turn must buy the property cheaply enough to add his own commission when he sells to a collector.

THE BEST WAY: SELLING TO OTHER COLLECTORS

Usually the best way to get top dollar for your material is by *reaching out directly to other collectors.* Some people do so by taking out their own ads in the stamp press, offering a detailed description of their holdings and quoting a price. If you belong to a stamp club, you might, through personal contact, find a buyer.

The other way is to dispose of your stamps at public auction, where wholesalers, retailers and collectors bids competitively. You do run the risk of having to accept low bids. But the auction route saves you time and effort. Also, a good auction gallery will put your stamps on display to thousands of potential buyers.

The gallery will carefully evaluate the condition of your stamp, describe it accurately, make a photograph (if necessary) for the catalogue, and strive to sell it at the highest possible price, since the gallery usually earns 20 percent of the price realized. One auctioneer, Frank Knina, 150 Nassau Street, Suite 1114-17, New York, N.Y. 10038, advertises that he will accept any lot with a minimum value of $100 and sell it at 10 percent commission, plus a $1 handling charge. But the question is: Will he get top dollar for your holdings?

SELLING BY AUCTION

Deal with members of the American Stamp Dealers Association who advertise regularly in the stamp press. Don't worry about sending your stamps by mail. Registered mail costs only 95 cents extra, and it is very safe.

Check the prices realized of auction houses that may be selling material similar to yours. This gives you an idea of what yours will bring.

The kind of material you have determines where to sell. I

recommend that you start with U.S. stamps, and this country is certainly the best market to sell it. But if you have German stamps, Germany is the best market, and you should check for auction houses there. British Commonwealth material does well here in the United States, but it may do better in England, or in Australia, and with a little checking around you can locate auction galleries there.

If you deal with a large, established auction gallery, here's what will happen. Write or call the gallery, describe what you have, and follow their instructions. In general, you will be asked to send the material, well-packed, by registered mail. From then on, the stamps will be protected by the gallery's insurance policy. You will be asked to approve some type of written consignment agreement.

The typical gallery holds sales several times a year. Your money, 80 percent of the winning bid realizations, will be sent to you five weeks after the date of the auction.

If you have a large collection that you prefer to sell intact to a single buyer, or if you need an immediate sale, ask the gallery whether they have a "private treaty" service. If they do, the gallery will appraise the value of the collection and seek a buyer. Sales can often be consummated in a few weeks, and your check is then sent immediately.

Via the private treaty route, if your property is sold for $5,000 or more, the gallery takes a 12½ percent commission; if the collection sells for $1,000 to $5,000, the gallery charges 15 percent; and it takes 17½ percent on materials sold for $1,000 or less. In all cases, the commission is lower than the standard 20 percent for auctions, because the gallery did not have to incur the expense of printing descriptions and photos of your properties in its catalogue.

If you need money in a hurry, let the gallery know. Most large galleries will advance you from 50 to 60 percent of the "gross expectation" immediately.

Also, a gallery can give you an appraisal of the worth of your material. The usual minimum charge for an appraisal is 2½ percent of the estimated value of your collection, with a minimum fee of $10. This fee will be waived if you allow the gallery to handle your material for sale.

What happens if you put your stamps up for auction and, by some quirk, the winning bids are so low that you stand to lose money? This is highly unlikely, but it is not impossible.

You can protect yourself. One way is to enter a bid for your own material, which establishes a minimum "floor." Be careful not to bid too high! You might have to buy your own stamps back, and pay the gallery a 20 percent commission to boot. This is preferable to letting someone else buy them for next to nothing because you can then try selling them at another auction. As I've said before, anything goes at an auction, and prices can swing rather unpredictably.

Perhaps a more sensible means of protecting your interests is the "guarantee plan" offered by a few galleries (H.R. Harmer is one). They will guarantee that you receive a certain amount for your collection, providing that you pay them a type of insurance premium of $2.50 for every $100 worth of guarantee.

HOW THE GUARANTEE PLAN WORKS

Let's see how this works. Suppose the gallery guarantees your collection for $20,000. Based on 2½ percent per $100 guaranteed, the gallery will charge you $500 for this insurance. It will also deduct its standard 20 percent auction commission from the gross proceeds. So based on a $20,000 guaranteed gross, the gallery will deduct $4,000 for commission and $500 for its guarantee fee, leaving you an "assured net" of $15,500. If you accept the guarantee plan, here are two possible results:

1. If the collection sells for $22,000, the guarantee was not

really necessary. Normally, without the guarantee, the gallery would subtract $4,400 for its commission, and leave you a net of $17,600. But in this case, it also deducts the $500 guarantee fee, reducing your net proceeds to $17,100. Still, it was a comfortable feeling to know that you were guaranteed at least $15,500.

2. What if the auction bidders are in a bearish mood? Suppose your entire collection sells for a gross of only $16,000? Without the guarantee, you would receive only $12,800. With the guarantee, you would still get your guaranteed figure of $15,500. By spending $500 on this form of insurance, you gain $2,700.

I believe that the auction route is usually the best means of disposing of your stamp properties. If, after personal experience, you arrive at the same conclusion, I suggest that you take certain precautions.

WHAT YOUR FAMILY SHOULD KNOW ABOUT YOUR STAMPS

It may not be pleasant to think about this now, but should you die and leave substantial assets in your stamp portfolio, your heirs may not be aware of the portfolio's value. To the person unfamiliar with philately, a collection worth thousands of dollars may appear to be a worthless assortment of little pieces of paper, stored in an album or in glassine envelopes. If you have invested regularly for a number of years, these little pieces of paper could be worth more than your house.

Your family should be made aware of the value of your stamp collection. If you deal regularly with an auction gallery in acquiring your stamps, you might consider allowing the same gallery to dispose of your philatelic estate. This is a simple matter. You can draft a provision in your will, or a codicil to your will, which reads: "I direct that the services of (name of gallery) of (city and state) be retained to appraise and sell my philatelic properties for such compensation as is customarily paid therefor."

In addition, you can leave brief written instructions for your family lawyer or heirs telling them how to arrange for the auction sale of your stamps.

SELLING PIECEMEAL

This may seem obvious, but always keep in mind that you needn't sell all of your stamps at once. At any time—perhaps to help finance your children's way through college, to pay for a long-desired vacation, or to meet regular expenses during your retirement years—you can sell off a portion of your portfolio.

Let us suppose that by age forty you had accumulated $10,000 worth of rare stamps. If they appreciate at a rate of 12 percent a year, they will triple to $30,000 in ten years, and to $90,000 by the time you are 60 years old. If your stamps are appreciating at a rate higher than bank savings, it would be silly to convert all of them into cash, providing you need only part of the proceeds. There are auction sales throughout the year. Most galleries will accept for sale any single stamp worth $50 or more, or a collection of stamps worth $200 or more. Why sell more than you need to?

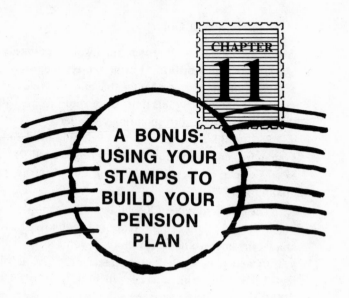

A BONUS: USING YOUR STAMPS TO BUILD YOUR PENSION PLAN

In this brief final chapter, I want to offer you a bonus, an investment idea with exciting potential.

Are you familiar with the Keogh Plan? If not, I urge you to learn about it. This federal pension law is named after its legislative sponsor, Eugene J. Keogh, a former Democratic representative of Brooklyn. The plan came into effect in 1962, but it was liberalized in 1974, and here are the principal points that will interest you.

1. If you are employed, but not covered by a pension plan, the government now allows you to set up your own retirement plan. You can contribute each year as much as 15 percent of your annual income, up to a limit of $1,500. The exciting feature of this plan is that it allows you to skim the money "off the top"; it is *tax deductible* from your income. In other words, much of the money

you use to build up a retirement fund would ordinarily be paid to Uncle Sam on April 15. Furthermore, interest or dividends earned from this plan are not taxable until you retire and begin to make withdrawals. By this time, since your income will be lower, the tax bite will be correspondingly smaller.

2. A similar Keogh Plan for self-employed individuals is even more generous. You can make tax-sheltered savings of up to $7,500 a year, or 15 percent of your annual income, whichever amount is less.

The standard type of Keogh Plan is a savings account with a bank. Suppose you are 35 years old, employed, and have an annual income of $10,000 or more. If you contribute $1,500 per year to your plan, by the time you reach age 65 you will have put in $45,000, but bank interest will build this up to more than $180,000. If you elect to receive the benefits on a monthly basis for ten years, you would receive (in addition to Social Security) $2,137 per month.

If you are self-employed, the benefits can be even greater. Suppose you put away $7,500 per year for 20 years. At normal bank interest, the $150,000 you invest would earn an additional $182,000. You could retire on $29,450 a year for the next 20 years.

Why am I telling you all this in a book about investment in rare stamps? Because the Keogh Plan is still quite new, and its multiple ramifications are yet to be explored. Under a little-noticed section of this legislation, a few commercial banks have set up trusts for self-employed individuals to *direct the investment* of their own tax-sheltered pension money. The Plymouth Home National Bank of Brockton, Mass., allows each participant to make his own investments in such widely divergent areas as stocks, bonds, mutual funds, and savings accounts. The bank serves as the trustee for these assets.

It is important to understand that, under a Keogh Plan, you must have a trustee. These assets must be kept away from your jurisdiction until you retire—usually age 65, but no earlier than age 59 and a half and no later than age 70 and a half. And thus far, the IRS will only allow a bank to serve as the trustee of a Keogh Plan.

If bank savings build up so dramatically over a period of years, you can imagine the fortune that one might build with rare stamps that are appreciating at 15 percent a year.

Do rare stamps qualify as legitimate investments under the Keogh Plan? Yes and no.

I recently called a Keogh Plan specialist with the IRS in Washington. He said that stamps, fine art, old coins and anything else technically *do qualify,* providing that one has documentation to show that these assets are acquired at fair market value, and that they do, indeed, appreciate in value. I believe we have made a forceful case for stamps in this book.

Although the IRS would approve of stamps, the next step is to find a trustee. To my knowledge, no bank, although it is legally allowed to do so, has yet seen fit to include rare stamps and other collectibles in its Keogh Plan.

"Anything is possible," I was told by Paul Henderson of the Plymouth Home National Bank in Brockton.

He says that he has considered the idea of rare coins and other collectibles, but the bank's board of directors hasn't given the green light at this writing.

I predict that it's merely a matter of time. Once bank officers are made aware of the potential of rare stamps, they can—by a simple administrative decision—make them eligible under the Keogh Plan.

Here is how it could work. You would arrange through a bank to set up your personal Keogh Plan. You would have to deposit cash in this account (up to $1,500 per year if you are an employee, and up to $7,500 per year if you are self-employed). At the same time, the bank would reserve a safety deposit box in your name, and retain custody of the key. You would spot a particular stamp at auction, or for sale in some other manner, that has a history of appreciating in value. You would then direct the bank to purchase the stamp for you with the funds that you have deposited.

In the case of an auction, you would have to make a winning bid, and once this is done, direct the gallery to send the invoice to your bank for payment. This must be done, because the trustee must carry out all investments in your behalf. The stamps can be sent to you first for your inspection before you forward them to the bank for safekeeping.

Mr. Henderson tells me that if such a plan were approved by his bank this service could be performed by the bank for a reasonable fee.

Other banks that already allow investors to direct their own Keogh Plan are the Security National Bank of Denver and the National Bank of Georgia. They, too, presently limit investments to stocks, bonds, mutual funds, and savings accounts.

I believe that in time more banks will allow such investor-directed plans, and then liberalize the procedure one step further to permit investments in rare stamps, coins, and fine art.

Until this happens, I suggest that you look into the possibility of setting up a Keogh Plan as soon as possible. You can begin with a savings account. Even though bank savings don't appreciate as rapidly as rare stamps, remember that you are investing money that might ordinarily be paid to the IRS in taxes. Once you have set up your Keogh Plan, keep abreast of new developments with reference to this new law. Ask your bank trustee if the plan has been liberalized.

And remember: The Keogh Plan is *flexible*. Part of your assets can be kept in bank savings, another part can be invested in bonds, and another portion can go into rare stamps—that way you won't be putting all of your eggs into one basket. The important thing is to start taking advantage of this marvelous tax shelter. It can make a world of difference in your life style when you retire.

To dramatize this, let's take a theoretical case illustrated in a Prentice-Hall newsletter devoted to personal and professional tax savings. The person was self-employed and was able to contribute

$7,500 per year to his Keogh Plan. Since he was in the 50 percent tax bracket, he immediately saved $3,720 per year in taxes, by "siphoning off" $7,500 into the Keogh Plan. Over a twenty-five-year period he had put his contributions into investments that averaged a before-tax return of only 6 percent (3 percent after taxes). Under an unsheltered investment plan, he would wind up with $141,950. With the Keogh Plan, he would accumulate $436,170.

We are talking about investments that offer a return of 6 percent. Imagine the benefits from rare stamps that grow in value by 12 percent or 15 percent per year!

CONCLUSION

I can think of no better way to conclude this book than to quote from the November 1901 issue of *The Metropolitan Philatelist:*

> Stamp collecting is an interesting amusement, a profitable business, and an open field for speculation. Speculators have always been and will always be; *the bright ones* will select suitable issues and will have money enough to buy all that are offered and will sell out at a large profit.
>
> Successful men will have weak imitators who buy *without knowledge* and will sell at a loss. But stamp collecting will go right on affording amusement to millions, business to hundreds, and fortunes to a few.

Remember my saying earlier, "Knowledge is power." Learn something about philately: its romance, its history, and—above all—its price structure.

In a recent article about investing in fine art, *Forbes* quoted an art dealer, John Richardson, who said: "There is a paradox here. For people who buy art out of an obsession—true collectors—art usually turns out to be a good investment. Whereas people who buy primarily as an investment nearly always end up losing money." Collectors, says *Forbes,* "instinctively buy well," because they "invariably become experts in their field." The magazine cites the case of taxi tycoon Robert Scull, who paid less than $1,000 each for what he considered to be his most important works of modern art, and in October 1973 auctioned off just 20 percent of his collection for a record $2.2 million.

The lesson is clear, I think. If you hope to profit from investments in rare stamps, do become a collector. Specialize in a country or two. Focus upon the classics of the country; those that were issued long ago, and have a lengthy track record.

You can go out right now and purchase the stamps that I recommend in this book, and I think you would stand an excellent chance of making good capital gains. But remember something else I said earlier: Don't place blind faith in anyone else. Not even me. It's *your* money.

Accept advice, but learn to make your own decisions.

This books offers you enough information to start you on the road toward becoming a knowledgeable collector/investor. Summing up, take the following steps:

1. Identify those classic stamps that are gaining in value by at least 10 percent yearly (consult Chapter Three).

2. Become familiar with the price structure of the philatelic market (see Chapter Six).

3. Familiarize yourself with the many sources of buying stamps (see Chapter Seven).

4. Don't be satisfied with stamps that are in less than Fine condition.

5. Develop a simple method of record-keeping and a safe means of storing your stamps (see Chapter Nine).

6. Be prepared to hold your stamps for the long-term, to insure maximum return on your investment. Make provisions in your will for the proper disposal of these precious assets, just in case. Properly chosen stamps have consistently outpaced the cost of living, stocks, mutual funds, and bank savings. Be patient. Give them time to grow in value.

7. Don't overspend. Decide how much you can comfortably afford to invest for the long term. Work out a budget (perhaps with a separate checking account) and invest regularly.

As you become familiar with the stamp world, you will find that there are numerous fringe benefits to this form of collecting / investing. Enjoy the sheer pleasure of possessing these antique miniature works of art. Enjoy the social aspect. Last summer, for example, there was a Caribbean and South American cruise on the Cunard Line ship *Adventurer,* with stamp experts, lectures, slide shows, and visits to stamp shops and post offices at each port of call.

If you go abroad, you'll find fascinating postal museums in Brussels, Cairo, Helsinki, Paris, London, Budapest, Tokyo. The Postal Museum of France on the boulevard de Vaugirard in Paris is one of the world's richest sources of postal history, with items that date back to the arrival of the Romans. The National Postal Museum in London on King Edward Street includes a splendid forty-six-volume collection of nineteenth-century British stamps and the original documents that pertain to Rowland Hill's invention of the postage stamp.

Here in the United States, don't miss the National Stamp Collection—12 million items—at the Museum of History and Technology of the Smithsonian Institution. There are always numerous philatelic exhibits, conventions and auctions which you can attend. If your community has a stamp club, you will learn a great deal from your fellow philatelists, and you may well develop some warm friendships. One midwestern bank president recently commented that he found it quite "therapeutic" to pore over his stamps and auction catalogues after a hard day at the office—just as the late President Roosevelt did.

Your stamp interests might also provide one more pleasant bridge between your children and you. Buy your son or daughter a beginner's album and a few dollars' worth of inexpensive stamps. Together, visit local stamp stores, exhibits, or auctions.

Perhaps the best feature of rare stamps is that they require attention only when *you* have the desire to buy or sell. Otherwise, like fine wine, they are content to rest quietly in some safe, dark place—growing rarer and more precious with the years.

INDEX